GOD

THE BIBLE IN A NUTSHELL

SIGNS

Donald Henderson

DONALD
HENDERSON

REDEMPTION◆PRESS

Published by Redemption Press, PO Box 427, Enumclaw, WA 98022.

ISBN 13: 978-1-63232-118-3
Library of Congress Catalog Card Number: 2006941011

TABLE OF CONTENTS

(Major supporting scriptures are indicated by an arrow.)

PREFACE

Seven years ago I decided to continue writing a book I had begun several years earlier. I was at a point of career uncertainty and was house-sitting for a couple months after living in an old Chevy van for more than a year.

It seemed likely that finishing the book was what the Lord intended as a means of bringing me some kind of an income. I had even been enjoying a certain level of inspiration. One morning as I sat down at the computer to write, the Lord told me to stop and gather together all of my Christian books. At the time, only about a dozen of them were available to me. But, I did as I was told.

God then told me to take the books that had really blessed me and put them in a pile to the right. I was to take the books that had *not* blessed me or that I could not even manage to get started reading and place them to the left. I obeyed. There were about half-a-dozen books in each pile. The Lord then said, "The books on the right were written to bless people; those on the left were written to make money. Which do you want to write?"

Without waiting for an answer, because He knew what was in my heart, God told me to put the computer away. I did not know if He was just putting the book on hold for a while or whether I would never write again. Within a few weeks I was, once more, living in my van. At the Lord's direction, relative to the story of the rich young ruler (below), I had spent my IRA money on an evangelism trip to the streets of Manhattan, New York, and on a donation to a missionary outreach in Russia.

Now I replayed the words of those scriptures in my mind:

16 And behold, there came a man up to Him, saying, Teacher, what excellent and perfectly and essentially good deed must I do to possess eternal life?

17And He said to him, Why do you ask Me about the perfectly and essentially good? There is only One Who is good [perfectly and essentially]—God. If you would enter into the Life, you must continually keep the commandments.

18He said to Him, What sort of commandments? [Or, which ones?] And Jesus answered, You shall not kill, You shall not commit adultery, You shall not steal, You shall not bear false witness,

19Honor your father and your mother, and, You shall love your neighbor as [you do] yourself.

20The young man said, I have observed all these from my youth; what still do I lack?

21Jesus answered him, If you would be perfect [that is, have that spiritual maturity which accompanies self-sacrificing character], go and sell what you have and give to the poor, and you will have riches in heaven; and come, be My disciple [side with My party and follow Me].

²²But when the young man heard this, he went away sad (grieved and in much distress), for he had great possessions.

²³And Jesus said to His disciples, Truly I say to you, it will be difficult for a rich man to get into the kingdom of heaven.
—Matthew 19:16–23 (AMP)

I spent the next seven years living in my van while on a mission and prayer walk on the streets and in the marketplaces of a suburb in Northwestern United States. I did not have the support of any church or missions board. I lived completely by faith, moving as the Lord directed.

The rules God gave were that I would ask no one for anything, or even drop hints as to my needs. I had only what was given voluntarily to me, as God provided. I was allowed to tell people what I was doing and how I was living, but only as led by the Holy Spirit.

I spent my days listening to God, interceding in a variety of ways, and encouraging believers, many of whom had no church or fellowship, and telling unbelievers about Jesus. The Lord also did some wonderful healing as He directed me to anoint the sick with oil in the name of Jesus.

It was during this time that God taught me much of what is written in this book. Just recently He put me in an apartment and is directing me to record and share the lessons I learned from Him during my years walking by His side through the highways and byways of life.

ACKNOWLEDGMENTS

I thank God Almighty for His inspiration and guidance in writing this book. I acknowledge that He alone is the Source of all blessings that may result from it.

I wish to express thanks to my parents, Howard G. Henderson (the late) and Adele L. Henderson, for their inspiring examples of persevering faithfully in the midst of adversity. I also thank my siblings, DeVere Henderson, Phyllis Henderson, and Stephen Henderson, for their support and encouragement over the years.

I wish to commend my sons, Jeffrey, Jared, and Joshua for persevering and achieving admirable goals during some very difficult years.

I am grateful to Christopher and Candace Ray for encouraging me to write this book and for their obedience to the Lord in the many significant ways that they have helped me.

I am also grateful for the sustaining support and kindness of Edward Welch, Thomas and LaDonna Gates, Ronald and

Sharon Garceau, Arturo and Adrea Whirt, Perry and Jan Olson, Troy and Kimberly Hedrick, the Stephen and Helen Howell family, and Alfred Allen and Gladys Medina.

I wish to express thanks to all others who encouraged and supported me in various ways during my missionary journey and writing efforts.

INTRODUCTION

One day during the summer between my freshman and sophomore years of high school I was watching television at home alone in my living room. I tuned in a crusade being conducted by Billy Graham and began watching. Being at a point of desperation, I knelt and prayed to receive Jesus Christ as my Savior. It is not easy to talk about this event in my life without feeling tremendous emotion, even though that day is now forty-two years in the past.

Just after my prayer, I soon began to enjoy a new intimacy with God, which included His comfort and answered prayer. However, I did fall under the sway, in some measure, to the now even more popular, blasphemous heresy that Jesus was "just" another teacher and a good man. I did continue to live a clean and moral life and to be faithful to my understanding of what God expected of me. In my senior year of high school I began to experience a hunger and longing for Him, just as if I had never known or experienced Him at all.

This agonizing emptiness and longing for Christ continued as I entered my first year at one of the United States service academies. Here, we were all issued copies of the *New Testament*. My roommate and I decided to set aside a little time each evening when we would separately read a portion of it. The Scriptures were enough comfort and peace to let me know that I was headed in the right direction, but my intense longing for God continued.

In the summer between my fourth class (freshman) and third class (sophomore) years, our class took a field trip to several different military installations across the country. I took every opportunity to visit churches as I continued my desperate search to know my Creator. I visited a variety of Protestant churches, the Roman Catholic Church, and the Latter Day Saints tabernacle in Salt Lake City. I came to the conclusion that God was not in any of the churches. I remembered the words of Jesus, which I had read in the *New Testament* and that my father had once quoted to me:

> ^{6} Jesus said to him, I am the Way and the Truth and the Life; no one comes to the Father except by (through) Me.
>
> —John 14:6 (AMP)

I also remembered hearing Billy Graham say that the only place where God could be found was in the Person of Jesus Christ. My soul yearned for an opportunity to attend a Billy Graham Crusade. I thought that if I could be physically present I would receive whatever was lacking in a television evangelism experience. What I did not understand was that I had received a New Life, Jesus Christ Himself, when I had prayed four years earlier. What God was really after was that I recall the truth about what I had received and always remember the truth of just Who He is. He is Emmanuel or "God with us" and nothing less.

> ²¹She will bear a Son, and you shall call His name Jesus [the Greek form of the Hebrew Joshua, which means Savior], for He will save His people from their sins [that is, prevent them from failing and missing the true end and scope of life, which is God].
> ²²All this took place that it might be fulfilled which the Lord had spoken through the prophet,
> ²³Behold, the virgin shall become pregnant and give birth to a Son, and they shall call His name Emmanuel—which, when translated, means, God with us.
> —Matthew 1:21–23 (AMP)

He is God Himself, come in the form of a man to reveal the character of the Father to us all!

> ⁵Let this same attitude and purpose and [humble] mind be in you which was in Christ Jesus: [Let Him be your example in humility:]
> ⁶Who, although being essentially one with God and in the form of God [possessing the fullness of the attributes which make God God], did not think this equality with God was a thing to be eagerly grasped or retained,
> ⁷But stripped Himself [of all privileges and rightful dignity], so as to assume the guise of a servant (slave), in that He became like men and was born a human being.
> ⁸And after He had appeared in human form, He abased and humbled Himself [still further] and carried His obedience to the extreme of death, even the death of the cross!
> —Philippians 2:5–8 (AMP)

I had received a New Life-form, now living in the depths of my being, and it was very important that I appreciate just Who I had received. This New Life-form was, as Jesus said of Himself and of His kingdom, "not of this world," but utterly extraterrestrial in nature.

> 23He said to them, You are from below; I am from above. You are of this world (of this earthly order); I am not of this world.
>
> —John 8:23 (AMP)

> 16 They are not of the world (worldly, belonging to the world), [just] as I am not of the world.
>
> —John 17:16 (AMP)

> 36Jesus answered, My kingdom (kingship, royal power) belongs not to this world. If My kingdom were of this world, My followers would have been fighting to keep Me from being handed over to the Jews. But as it is, My kingdom is not from here (this world); [it has no such origin or source].
> 37Pilate said to Him, Then You are a King? Jesus answered, You say it! [You speak correctly!] For I am a King. [Certainly I am a King!] This is why I was born, and for this I have come into the world, to bear witness to the Truth. Everyone who is of the Truth [who is a friend of the Truth, who belongs to the Truth] hears and listens to My voice.
>
> —John 18:36–37 (AMP)

He is nothing like anything this world has ever seen, and that is what He came to show us.

When I returned to the academy at the beginning of the academic school year I found a surprise on the squadron bulletin board. It was a sign-up list for a bus trip to a Billy Graham crusade in a nearby city. Of course, I put my name on the list and was among those going forward to receive Christ at the closing invitation.

I had peace on the bus trip home. As I walked between my scheduled academic classes, I had new joy in just looking at the sky or other parts of God's creation. I found myself once again spontaneously praying to my God. The Billy Graham Evangelistic Association sent me my first Bible study lesson, with instructions to complete it and mail it back to them. As I did so, they sent me another and another until I had completed all four lessons of their *New Believer's Study* package.

Through those studies I received an understanding of the importance of knowing and not forgetting the true identity of Jesus. I received a much greater comprehension of the significance of His death and Resurrection, which had provided my salvation from a state of *separation* from God to a place of having a relationship with Him.

Each Friday evening I received a visit from a cadet in the class ahead of mine for a time of fellowship. When my cadet came, I had never met him before, but he had been told of my recent decision to follow Jesus Christ. His visits had a great impact on my life, bringing encouragement. He always had his *New Testament* in his pocket. I recognized this to be a significant practice for a person who takes their walk with God seriously. Since that time I have made it a habit to always have a *New Testament* or an entire Bible with me wherever I go.

The importance of the new life cannot be overstated because it is the very essence of our salvation from an eternal exclusion from God's Kingdom, and that is certainly the greatest measure of Hell. Salvation is not merely an acknowledgment of who Jesus is. One must first recognize the wickedness and disobedience of his or her present state, then have a desire to make an about-face and live life God's way. It must be realized that eternal separation from God is what is deserved, but a merciful and gracious Father is offering us a pardon.

Let me explain it like this: Five prisoners are on death row for horrible crimes that they have separately committed. The Governor sends each a "get out of jail free" card that says, "We have a law in this land that two people cannot be punished for the same offense. Last night I allowed my only son to be executed in your place. Since he was an absolutely perfect man, his death is sufficient punishment for all of you. If you will just remorsefully admit your guilt, present this card to the guard, and state your desire to have a new life with intent to live as my perfect son did, you will walk free. Additionally, we will establish for you a new life and a new identity and give you all the assistance you need to walk in *newness of life*. We realize that there will be a learning process as we teach you to walk in newness of life, and that is understood."

One prisoner thanks the messenger for the pardon and walks free to a changed life and an eternal reward. The second prisoner replies, "I don't believe any of this stuff!" A third prisoner answers, "That's absurd! No governor would do that for a wicked man like me." The fourth prisoner says, "I'm a good person. I don't need a pardon when I've done nothing all that bad."

> [23]Since all have sinned and are falling short of the honor and glory which God bestows and receives.
>
> —Romans 3:23 (AMP)

The fifth casually answers, "I think I'll wait until the last minute," while ignoring that execution could come at any time, as an instantaneous and total surprise. Jesus stated that in the final analysis people will not suffer judgment because of the sins they committed, but only because they rejected His pardon!

> ¹⁸ He who believes in Him [who clings to, trusts in, relies on Him] is not judged [he who trusts in Him never comes up for judgment; for him there is no rejection, no condemnation—he incurs no damnation]; but he who does not believe (cleave to, rely on, trust in Him) is judged already [he has already been convicted and has already received his sentence] because he has not believed in and trusted in the name of the only begotten Son of God. [He is condemned for refusing to let his trust rest in Christ's name.]
>
> —John 3:18 (AMP)

Right before Jesus raised Lazarus from the dead He explained this plainly to Martha:

> ²³Jesus said to her, Your brother shall rise again.
> ²⁴Martha replied, I know that he will rise again in the resurrection at the last day.
> ²⁵Jesus said to her, I am [Myself] the Resurrection and the Life. Whoever believes in (adheres to, trusts in, and relies on) Me, although he may die, yet he shall live;
>
> —John 11:23–25 (AMP)

Eternal life is not an extension on existence delivered to us when we die. Eternal life is a person named Jesus, received only by repenting of sin and asking for Him. When this is done, a human becomes a holy temple of God, as Christ takes up residence within.

> [11]And this is that testimony (that evidence): God gave us eternal life, and this life is in His Son.
> [12]He who possesses the Son has that life; he who does not possess the Son of God does not have that life.
>
> —1 John 5:11–12 (AMP)

Receiving His New Life is wonderful, and is the starting point of a lifelong adventure and a process of transformation. This starting point is a prerequisite to realizing the maximum application and potential of the lessons that follow.

CHAPTER 1

WHAT'S IT ALL ABOUT?

Suffering is a reality that everyone must deal with at some point. It is one of the most common issues with God mentioned by unbelievers, especially those who oppose faith. Nearly every believer will be asked *why suffering exists* and will probably wonder himself why God, who is infinitely kind and loving, would create a universe, then allow it to fall into such a sorry state of pain and turmoil.

The Bible is not silent concerning God's purpose in creation, nor is it silent concerning the cause of suffering, nor its purpose in our lives. God's ultimate purpose in this and in all things is discussed in the book of Ephesians.

> [4]But God—so rich is He in His mercy! Because of and in order to satisfy the great and wonderful and intense love with which He loved us,
> [5]Even when we were dead (slain) by [our own] shortcomings and trespasses, He made us alive together in fellowship and in

union with Christ; [He gave us the very life of Christ Himself, the same new life with which He quickened Him, for] it is by grace (His favor and mercy which you did not deserve) that you are saved (delivered from judgment and made partakers of Christ's Salvation).

⁶And He raised us up together with Him and made us sit down together [giving us joint seating with Him] in the heavenly sphere [by virtue of our being] in Christ Jesus (the Messiah, the Anointed One).

⇨ ⁷He did this that He might clearly demonstrate through the ages to come the immeasurable (limitless, surpassing) riches of His free grace (His unmerited favor) in [His] kindness and goodness of heart toward us in Christ Jesus.

—Ephesians 2:4–7 (AMP)

⁵[This mystery] was never disclosed to human beings in past generations as it has now been revealed to His holy apostles (consecrated messengers) and prophets by the [Holy] Spirit.

⁶[It is this:] that the Gentiles are now to be fellow heirs [with the Jews], members of the same body and joint partakers [sharing] in the same divine promise in Christ through [their acceptance of] the glad tidings (the Gospel).

—Ephesians 3:5–6 (AMP)

⁹Also to enlighten all men and make plain to them what is the plan [regarding the Gentiles and providing for the Salvation of all men] of the mystery kept hidden through the ages and concealed until now in [the mind of] God Who created all things by Christ Jesus.

⇨ ¹⁰[The purpose is] that through the church the complicated, many-sided wisdom of God in all its infinite variety and innumerable aspects might now be made known to the angelic rulers and authorities (principalities and powers) in the heavenly sphere.

[11]This is in accordance with the terms of the eternal and timeless purpose which He has realized and carried into effect in [the person of] Christ Jesus our Lord,

[12]In Whom, because of our faith in Him, we dare to have the boldness (courage and confidence) of free access (an unreserved approach to God with freedom and without fear).

—Ephesians 3:9–12 (AMP)

His purpose in the creation, then, is to obtain for Himself a bride in a meaningful freewill love relationship and to make known His desire or need for this kind of relationship. He intends that all created beings will see attributes of Himself that could only be revealed through a medium that gives them meaning—that is, a fallen creation, a lost and dying world.

Sacrificial love, grace, and mercy were for the first time displayed as God exercised them in an environment created for the purpose of revealing His character to His own. Even this very act itself further displays His love—His intense desire to share Himself with not just His bride, but with all His creation through the revelation of His character. And doing all this cost Him dearly:

[16]For God so greatly loved and dearly prized the world that He [even] gave up His only begotten (unique) Son, so that whoever believes in (trusts in, clings to, relies on) Him shall not perish (come to destruction, be lost) but have eternal (everlasting) life.

—John 3:16 (AMP)

Also, His wrath and judgment are revealed in a way previously unknown.

In this revelation of His character we, the church, have a center-stage role as His Bride; we are the recipients of His love exhibited. In this demonstration of love He will share His throne with us in a union of intimacy for all eternity (Ephesians 2:6, previously quoted). This was His plan long before the creation.

> [4]Even as [in His love] He chose us [actually picked us out for Himself as His own] in Christ before the foundation of the world, that we should be holy (consecrated and set apart for Him) and blameless in His sight, even above reproach, before Him in love.
> [5]For He foreordained us (destined us, planned in love for us) to be adopted (revealed) as His own children through Jesus Christ, in accordance with the purpose of His will [because it pleased Him and was His kind intent]—
> [6][So that we might be] to the praise and the commendation of His glorious grace (favor and mercy), which He so freely bestowed on us in the Beloved.
> [11]In Him we also were made [God's] heritage (portion) and we obtained an inheritance; for we had been foreordained (chosen and appointed beforehand) in accordance with His purpose, Who works out everything in agreement with the counsel and design of His [own] will,
> —Ephesians 1:4–6, 11 (AMP)

This was God's intent in sending His Son to redeem us. To illustrate it, let me share a short story. Once there was a cartoon that showed a woman in a wedding dress primping in front of a mirror. The caption read: "Just think! In less than an hour I will be Mrs. What's-his-name!" It is doubtful that anyone would envy her future husband.

What could this woman's motive in marriage be? Is she just looking for someone with a paycheck to cover all of her living expenses? Such a motive with no desire for a love relationship would be much like that of a prostitute. Or is she just in love with domestic life and maintaining her own household? God continually rebuked Israel for such motives, as did Jesus. We too must stay aware of the pitfalls of giving too high a priority on what we expect God to do for *us,* to the benefits of church life and even the joy of being used in ministry. Relationship with the Lord must always come first.

Many, many years ago the Lord rebuked me with the question, "Who is going to be your God? Am I going to be your God, or is *ministry* going to be your God?" In Revelation 2:4–5, Jesus gave stern warning concerning the dangers of replacing our original love for Him with something else. The Jews very much loved being religious. They even loved knowing and keeping the Law. In fact, they excelled at it! Yet Jesus accused them of honoring God with their lips while having hearts that were far from Him.

It is so easy to become overly preoccupied with ministry to others and, even worse, to be obsessed with attaining to someone else's misguided standard of success. The only standard for success is obedience to Christ in all things with a heart filled with love for the Master. What He does with our act of obedience to bring about a certain result is His business only. This requires that one keenly recognize His voice, which may seem an overwhelming and bothersome task for someone not interested in any such thing in the first place!

However, Jesus did say, "My sheep know My voice," (John 10:27). He also told us that in the judgment *many* (not a few) will come to Him proclaiming the success of their ministry and that His response will be, "Get out of here; I have never known you [author's paraphrase of Matthew 7:23]!" No small wonder that there will be wailing and gnashing of teeth as those who confidently considered they had settled the question of their own eternal salvation long before this begin to be sentenced without appeal to an eternity without God. Imagine the anguish as they begin to scream through clenched teeth, "What do you mean? I served You all of those years."

In 1 Corinthians 3:12–13 the destruction by fire of wood, hay, and stubble is discussed. It illustrates the key point here: Having false motives renders any good work we do as nothing but flammable wood, hay, and stubble.

Several years ago a man in southern California had a vision. He saw a woman in a wedding dress. The dress was soiled and wrinkled; the woman's hair uncombed and matted. Her face was bruised. She had been greatly abused. Then the Lord told him, "This is my church—and those who did this to her are her leaders."

Ephesians 4:11–14 says that the Lord has given leaders to the church in order to bring His people to maturity and to protect them from men who would mislead and harm them. Three times in John 15:13–15, Jesus refers to us as "friends." He later tells Peter how He expects him to act out his friendship:

> [15]When they had eaten, Jesus said to Simon Peter, Simon, son of John, do you love Me more than these [others do—with reasoning, intentional, spiritual devotion, as one loves the Father]? He said to Him, Yes, Lord, You know that I love You

[that I have deep, instinctive, personal affection for You, as for a close friend]. He said to him, Feed My lambs.

¹⁶Again He said to him the second time, Simon, son of John, do you love Me [with reasoning, intentional, spiritual devotion, as one loves the Father]? He said to Him, Yes, Lord, You know that I love You [that I have a deep, instinctive, personal affection for You, as for a close friend]. He said to him, Shepherd, (tend) My sheep.

¹⁷He said to him the third time, Simon, son of John, do you love Me [with a deep, instinctive, personal affection for Me, as for a close friend]? Peter was grieved (was saddened and hurt) that He should ask him the third time, Do you love Me? And he said to Him, Lord, You know everything; You know that I love You [that I have a deep, instinctive, personal affection for You, as for a close friend]. Jesus said to him, Feed My sheep.

—John 21:15–17 (AMP)

Imagine a man planning a wedding. He loves his fiancée so much that he has suffered unspeakably just so that he can spend time with her (John 3:16). Now imagine he even *died* for her and was somehow brought back to life. He can hardly wait for the wedding day, but he must first leave the area for a while in order to prepare a place for her to live (John 14:2–3). He calls his good friend and trusts him to help her to prepare herself for the wedding while he is gone (Ephesians 4:11–13, Ephesians 5:24–27).

When the bridegroom returns he finds her bruised and abused, as described in the vision—all of this done by his "good friend." If you were the bridegroom, how would you feel about that friend? Your feelings might probably be a baffling combination of betrayed, bewildered, and outraged! Who would want to be in that friend's shoes, especially if the bridegroom were one with unlimited authority? Likewise, no one would want to reap the "reward" of any leader who has prostituted the Bride of Jesus Christ for his own gains of fame, wealth, or fleshly lust.

Suffering entered the human race (1 Corinthians 15:21–22) and the created universe of space and time (Romans 8:18–23) when Adam disobeyed God (Genesis 3:15–18). These same scriptures, as well as many others, promise that one day the time of suffering will end for those willing to follow Jesus on the narrow path that leads to Everlasting Life (Matthew 7:13). However, until then each believer is appointed his or her portion of suffering as allowed or determined by the Lord.

[21]When they had preached the good news (Gospel) to that town and made disciples of many of the people, they went back to Lystra and Iconium and Antioch,
[22]Establishing *and* strengthening the souls *and* the hearts of the disciples, urging *and* warning *and* encouraging them to stand firm in the faith, and [telling them] that it is through many hardships *and* tribulations we must enter the kingdom of God.

—Acts 14:21–22 (AMP)

The message of the gospel of Jesus Christ is not a theology of suffering. It is a message of hope, healing, and deliverance! This is what Jesus came to bring us, but it is certainly not a balanced biblical faith that claims all of those precious promises while ignoring a vast number of "promises" that many would consider not-quite-so precious. If we refuse to acknowledge their existence and fail to comprehend their purpose, we will always be confused and suffer stunted spiritual growth. Instead, let us seek true understanding of God's wondrous promises.

I knew an athletic coach who had a standard comment for athletes when giving them a particularly tough opponent to practice with: "You never get any stronger lifting straws," he would say. Similarly, you do not often see a massively muscular weightlifter working out with an empty barbell—unless he is recovering from an injury. If you want to build muscle you must put some weight on the bar. You must make it *hard* to lift, or else you will get no training benefit out of it. In the military, whenever anyone had an undesirable circumstance forced upon him the standard sarcastic quip was: "It builds character."

This fallen creation not only serves to manifest attributes of God heretofore not seen, but it is also a necessary ingredient in the process of building the character of Christ in us. *Opposition* is a necessary ingredient for building the muscle of strong Christian character. The process would be impossible, of course, without the operation of the Holy Spirit through the Blood of Jesus, but adversity is an ingredient that He uses to train us.

The Scriptures make it very clear that we are not redeemed from all suffering, but rather we are called to it! We should never make an effort to produce suffering; we are to resist the devil always. When we know that we are yielded to the Lord and the suffering seems unavoidable, we must bear it patiently. If we find the mind of God in our suffering, we can even experience a certain joy of yielding to Him in the middle of it all.

[20][After all] what kind of glory [is there in it] if, when you do wrong and are punished for it, you take it patiently? But if you bear patiently with suffering [which results] when you

do right and that is undeserved, it is acceptable and pleasing
to God.

²¹For even to this were you called [it is inseparable from
your vocation]. For Christ also suffered for you, leaving you
[His personal] example, so that you should follow in His
footsteps.

—1 Peter 2:20–21 (AMP)

We are not to shrink back from difficulties (Hebrews 10:38).
To do so is certainly not pleasing to God, and in fact *can* invoke
His wrath. When we courageously endure we prove outwardly
the sanctification that He is working in us within.

¹So, since Christ suffered in the flesh for us, for you, arm
yourselves with the same thought and purpose [patiently to
suffer rather than fail to please God]. For whoever has suffered in the flesh [having the mind of Christ] is done with
[intentional] sin [has stopped pleasing himself and the world,
and pleases God],

²So that he can no longer spend the rest of his natural life
living by [his] human appetites and desires, but [he lives] for
what God wills.

—1 Peter 4:1–2 (AMP)

²And we sent Timothy, our brother and God's servant in
[spreading] the good news (the Gospel) of Christ, to strength-
en and establish and to exhort and comfort and encourage
you in your faith,

³That no one [of you] should be disturbed and beguiled and
led astray by these afflictions and difficulties [to which I have
referred]. For you yourselves know that this is [unavoidable in
our position, and must be recognized as] our appointed lot.

WHAT'S IT ALL ABOUT?

⁴For even when we were with you, [you know] we warned you plainly beforehand that we were to be pressed with difficulties and made to suffer affliction, just as to your own knowledge it has [since] happened.

—1 Thessalonians 3:2–4 (AMP)

God does not produce suffering. Rather, there is a *ravenous creature* roaming the earth who does so continuously. In fact, that is his most treasured vocation! But, the Lord does precisely monitor his access to us, and even causes the otherwise horrible events he causes to work in our favor in the end (Romans 8:28).

⁸Be well balanced (temperate, sober of mind), be vigilant and cautious at all times; for that enemy of yours, the devil, roams around like a lion roaring [in fierce hunger], seeking someone to seize upon and devour.
⁹Withstand him; be firm in faith [against his onset—rooted, established, strong, immovable, and determined], knowing that the same (identical) sufferings are appointed to your brotherhood (the whole body of Christians) throughout the world.
¹⁰And after you have suffered a little while, the God of all grace [Who imparts all blessing and favor], Who has called you to His [own] eternal glory in Christ Jesus, will Himself complete and make you what you ought to be, establish and ground you securely, and strengthen, and settle you.

—1 Peter 5:8–10 (AMP)

More than once Scripture refers to us as *soldiers, athletes,* and *farmers.* Descriptions are also given of *boxing, wrestling, running,* and competing for a prize or a crown.

³Take [with me] your share of the hardships and suffering [which you are called to endure] as a good (first-class) soldier of Christ Jesus.

⁴No soldier when in service gets entangled in the enterprises of [civilian] life; his aim is to satisfy and please the one who enlisted him.

⁵And if anyone enters competitive games, he is not crowned unless he competes lawfully (fairly, according to the rules laid down).

⁶[It is] the hardworking farmer [who labors to produce] who must be the first partaker of the fruits.

⁷Think over these things I am saying [understand them and grasp their application], for the Lord will grant you full insight and understanding in everything.

⁸Constantly keep in mind Jesus Christ (the Messiah) [as] risen from the dead, [as the prophesied King] descended from David, according to the good news (the Gospel) that I preach.

⁹For that [Gospel] I am suffering affliction and even wearing chains like a criminal. But the Word of God is not chained or imprisoned!

¹⁰Therefore I [am ready to] persevere and stand my ground with patience and endure everything for the sake of the elect [God's chosen], so that they too may obtain [the] Salvation which is in Christ Jesus, with [the reward of] eternal glory.

¹¹The saying is sure and worthy of confidence: If we have died with Him, we shall also live with Him.

¹²If we endure, we shall also reign with Him. If we deny and disown and reject Him, He will also deny and disown and reject us.

—2 Timothy 2:3–12 (AMP)

WHAT'S IT ALL ABOUT?

When God calls on us to endure suffering, we must take care that we submit to it as to the discipline of a loving father (Hebrews 12:3–13). If an athletic coach sees potential in his first team and makes them practice harder and longer than the second team, it would be foolish to attribute it all to indifference or a grudge punishment. The book of Proverbs has a strong theme that a wise person appreciates honest and competent correction.

> [1]WHOEVER LOVES instruction and correction loves knowledge, but he who hates reproof is like a brute beast, stupid and indiscriminating.
>
> —Proverbs 12:1 (AMP)

> [20]A man who is held in honor and understands not is like the beasts that perish.
>
> —Psalm 49:20 (AMP)

We must also be careful to appreciate the fact that we are a part of this fallen creation for one lifetime only. We cannot build the muscle of Christian character once we have left this life and are in a place that has no weights to lift—no opposition or enemy of any kind. The character we leave this planet with is the full measure of character we will have for all eternity. It is one aspect of our crown and reward, and it will define our identities forever. It is the *measuring stick* of our "overcoming" in this life and is the gauge that defines our inheritance in accordance with the rich promises to the church so heavily emphasized in Revelation 2–3.

This does not mean that any part of an inheritance is obtained by our works, for Jesus said that the work God asks of us is to believe on the Messenger He sends (John 6:29). All of our inheritance is free! All that is required is that we yield to the process ordained by God to prepare us for all that He wants to give. This is why He sent the Holy Spirit to us! It is He who first convicts us of our need for Jesus and then leads us on to realize the fulfillment of our precious, blood-bought promises.

> [12]Now we have not received the spirit [that belongs to] the world, but the [Holy] Spirit Who is from God, [given to us] that we might realize and comprehend and appreciate the gifts [of divine favor and blessing so freely and lavishly] bestowed on us by God.
>
> —1 Corinthians 2:12 (AMP)

It behooves us to get to know our Comforter well and to cooperate with Him fully as He works to fulfill His mission here—to lead us into all that Jesus intends for us to have. The entire purpose of our lives is to cooperate fully with God as He molds us (and others) into what He wants us to be. We should do this out of a desire to please Him by becoming all that He intends us to be.

CHAPTER 2

DO YOU HAVE A PROMISE?

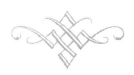

Asking a Christian if he has a promise might seem like a very uninformed question to some because everyone should know that we have an entire Bible full of promises. And that is true; we do! However, each promise has its proper place on a timeline, and God is the one who writes the schedule—not we.

He alone determines when each promise He's given is to be appropriated to an individual. All we have to do is obey, and the Holy Spirit does all that He can to lead us individually to receive the fullness of each promise at just the right time. Our being led to receive the promises of God is just the same as the Israelites being led to receive the Promised Land. Just as their grumbling about God's schedule and methods lengthened their stay in the wilderness, so will an unyielded heart interfere with His good plans for us. Just as those who had stubborn and complaining hearts of unbelief died in the wilderness, so must those same manifestations of self-determination that we have be put to death before we can enter into the fullness of all God has promised.

We must be yielded not only to His schedule and roadmap, but also to His commands relative to living an obedient and holy life before Him. We cannot expect God to fulfill His promises to us if we are willfully disobedient, or indifferent, or careless in regard to hearing and obeying His voice. He proved that this is so with the example of the ancient Israelites, who died in the wilderness because of their unbelief. They never saw fulfill-ment of the promises that God (who cannot lie) had made to them (Numbers 14:21–23). We should not fear that we cannot live up to the standard required for us to receive the promises. Rather, we should be certain that we cannot ourselves without His help.

> [34]Wait for and expect the Lord and keep and heed His way, and He will exalt you to inherit the land; [in the end] when the wicked are cut off, you shall see it.
>
> —Psalm 37:34 (AMP)

We may have a long wait from the time we receive a promise from God to the time of its fulfillment. In fact, more often than not this seems to be the case. While it is good to be indifferent to the timeframe of a promise's fulfillment, leaving that up to the Lord, we must not be indifferent to seeking His face and living a lifestyle that is pleasing to Him. To say, "He's got my address, and I'm going to do my own thing while I have to wait for Him to act," would not be at all right.

We may have some of our most severe tests during a *waiting period* and need His constant strength and assistance just to hold on. That is how it was for Noah, Abraham, Joseph, Moses, and the nation of Israel and David. This is the biblical pattern. God does not usually give us a promise for some great blessing that He intends to deliver the next morning. There is no need for it. Usually He will just give us a sweet surprise when least expected, and we'll recognize it as an intimate display of His lovingkindness toward us.

There are exceptions to this pattern, however, such as the incidents described in 1 Kings 13 and 2 Kings 7. These are minor incidents compared to the vast descriptions allotted to the lives of Abraham and the others. The truth is that God gives us promises so that we will have something to hold onto and to give us hope while we go through a horrendous and drawn out time of pruning and testing. It is as if He looks down on a Moses or a Joseph and says, "I have a position planned for this guy, but He is just not ready for it yet. He acts hastily and in his own strength and boasts prematurely on everything that I tell him. To put it briefly, he is impatient about everything. With the proper training, though, I think that I can have him ready for the time when he will be most needed. How can I help him to courageously endure the training and not give up? I know! I will tell him what I have planned for Him and the reward he will get if he does not give up."

The Lord then sets about instilling in us the qualities of Christian character commensurate with the position that He has planned for us. Scripture describes God's training plan this way:

[16]This is the agreement (testament, covenant) that I will set up and conclude with them after those days, says the Lord: I will imprint My laws upon their hearts, and I will

inscribe them on their minds (on their inmost thoughts and understanding),

—Hebrews 10:16 (AMP)

⁵Oh, that my ways were directed and established to observe Your statutes [hearing, receiving, loving, and obeying them]!
⁶Then shall I not be put to shame [by failing to inherit Your promises] when I have respect to all Your commandments.

—Psalm 119:5–6 (AMP)

³Be assured and understand that the trial and proving of your faith brings out endurance and steadfastness and patience.
⁴But let endurance and steadfastness and patience have full play and do a thorough work, so that you may be [people] perfectly and fully developed [with no defects], lacking in nothing.

—James 1:3–4 (AMP)

³⁵Do not, therefore, fling away your fearless confidence, for it carries a great and glorious compensation of reward.
³⁶For you have need of steadfast patience and endurance, so that you may perform and fully accomplish the will of God, and thus receive and carry away [and enjoy to the full] what is promised.

—Hebrews 10:35–36 (AMP)

We do not have to do an in-depth Scripture study to determine how to get everything we can from God. Instead, we should study to get all we can of *God Himself* and thus become everything that God wants us to be. Our walk is not about getting everything we can from God; rather it is about being certain that we give to Him all that we should. Romans 12:1 says that we should present our bodies as *living sacrifices* to God. It goes on to say that even this is not to be considered as some big deal or a great sacrificial deed; it is merely the *reasonable* thing for us to do in light of all that He has done for us. It is our reasonable service! And He has given us the wonderful, loving, and powerful Holy Spirit to lead us step by step into the righteousness of Christ so that we will not miss out on anything! We must, however, trust Him with the timeline, await His promised blessings, and obey Him in all things.

So then, what does it mean for a person to say that he has *"a promise from God"* if all of the promises in the Bible belong to every Christian anyway and will be fulfilled in this life or the next? What it means is that our personal and loving God Jehovah has in some way personally shown you a Bible promise because He wants you to hope in it as a means of drawing strength for the future. This is an important point.

> [18]Where there is no vision [no redemptive revelation of God], the people perish; but he who keeps the law [of God, which includes that of man]—blessed (happy, fortunate, and enviable) is he.
>
> —Proverbs 29:18 (AMP)

So then, to ask a man if he has *a promise* is to ask if he has a current vision. Has God added His anointing to some aspect of Bible-promised redemption so that faith is imparted to the heart? Has the Lord given a personal, faith-filled revelation of God's intent to fulfill the promise? Such a revelation may even include details of God's intended means of fulfillment or details depicting the result. The faith imparted to you to see the vision come to pass is a precious commodity—a priceless gift!

> ¹[OH, I know, I have been rash to talk out plainly this way to God!] I will [in my thinking] stand upon my post of observation and station myself on the tower or fortress, and will watch to see what He will say within me and what answer I will make [as His mouthpiece] to the perplexities of my complaint against Him.
> ²And the Lord answered me and said, Write the vision and engrave it so plainly upon tablets that everyone who passes may [be able to] read [it easily and quickly] as he hastens by.
> ³For the vision is yet for an appointed time and it hastens to the end [fulfillment]; it will not deceive or disappoint. Though it tarry, wait [earnestly] for it, because it will surely come; it will not be behindhand on its appointed day.
> ⁴Look at the proud; his soul is not straight or right within him, but the [rigidly] just and the [uncompromisingly] righteous man shall live by his faith and in his faithfulness.
>
> —Habakkuk 2:1–4 (AMP)

CHAPTER 3

A PATTERN FOR AUTHORITY

The great patriarchs of Scripture received promises, acted on them, and endured long periods of testing before receiving fulfillment of the promises. But even more powerful than *their* example is the clear doctrine of salvation that is the core, underlying theme of the entire Bible—the Old and New Testaments: patient obedience. The spirit of the world is not in agreement with concepts like *patient waiting* and *character-building*. Its emphasis is on obtaining the greatest degree of success in the least amount of time. Such success may be hollow and devoid of meaningful content, however. This is not the case in God's economy. Jesus is far more concerned with having quality emanate from the core than with superficial appearances.

John the Baptist gave a very stern warning in Matthew 3 to those who thought external trimmings were sufficient. He made it clear that being descendents of Abraham and wearing the garments prescribed in the Torah were not sufficient, either. A change in behavior and heart attitude is absolutely required.

John then affirmed *water baptism* as symbolic of an act of repentance. He went on to proclaim the arrival of the long-ago promised Messiah. This Messiah would offer the *only* cure for the wayward heart. He would baptize in the Holy Spirit and with fire! So there are three key experiences mentioned in the events detailed in Matthew, chapter 3:

1. Water
2. Holy Spirit
3. Fire

[8]Bring forth fruit that is consistent with repentance [let your lives prove your change of heart];

[9]And do not presume to say to yourselves, We have Abraham for our forefather; for I tell you, God is able to raise up descendants for Abraham from these stones!

[10]And already the ax is lying at the root of the trees; every tree therefore that does not bear good fruit is cut down and thrown into the fire.

[11]I indeed baptize you in (with) water because of repentance [that is, because of your changing your minds for the better, heartily amending your ways, with abhorrence of your past sins]. But He Who is coming after me is mightier than I, Whose sandals I am not worthy *or* fit to take off *or* carry; He will baptize you with the Holy Spirit and with fire.

[12]His winnowing fan (shovel, fork) is in His hand, and He will thoroughly clear out *and* clean His threshing floor and gather *and* store His wheat in His barn, but the chaff He will burn up with fire that cannot be put out.

—Matthew 3:8–12 (AMP)

Soon after these words were spoken, the Mighty Messiah arrived on the scene. John knew (John 3:30) that his own work was preparatory only, and that Jesus had come to take over. He was startled and bewildered when this Mighty One came to him to be baptized! When John protested, Jesus explained that this water baptism was necessary for them to do. He knew that He was about to begin His ministry. With His actions before man He wanted to paint a picture showing us the way. So, we would see in His actions all that is required of those who wish to receive the fullness of His redemptive work!

[13]Then Jesus came from Galilee to the Jordan to John to be baptized by him.

[14] But John protested strenuously, having in mind to prevent Him, saying, It is I who have need to be baptized by You, and do You come to me?

[15]But Jesus replied to him, Permit it just now; for this is the fitting way for [both of] us to fulfill all righteousness [that is, to perform completely whatever is right]. Then he permitted Him.

[16]And when Jesus was baptized, He went up at once out of the water; and behold, the heavens were opened, and he [John] saw the Spirit of God descending like a dove and alighting on Him.

[17]And behold, a voice from heaven said, This is My Son, My Beloved, in Whom I delight!

4:1 THEN JESUS was led (guided) by the [Holy] Spirit into the wilderness (desert) to be tempted (tested and tried) by the devil.

—Matthew 3:13–4:1 (AMP)

So John obeyed and baptized Jesus in water—the first requirement that Jesus insisted upon. The verse says that Jesus, "went up at once out of the water." He didn't linger at the baptism of repentance but went immediately on to the second requirement. He was immediately baptized in the Holy Spirit. Next Jesus was led into the wilderness to be tempted and tried.

This is the third step—a fiery experience for removing impurities and/or confirming purity prior to full qualification. As it was proclaimed in His infancy, the Father here proclaims that Jesus is His beloved Son. However, a father will not trust a son with his business until a certain level of maturity is reached. It was after being tested that the ministry of Jesus began. He preached repentance, announced the Kingdom of Heaven, and exercised authority over the powers of evil in healing and deliverance.

This three-step process was plainly foreshadowed in the requirements that Jehovah God laid out for the Hebrews. Compliance was essential to realizing victory over their enemies.

> [18]The Feast of Unleavened Bread you shall keep. Seven days you shall eat unleavened bread, as I commanded you, in the time of the month of Abib; for in the month of Abib you came out of Egypt.
> [22]You shall observe the Feast of Weeks, the firstfruits of the wheat harvest, and the Feast of Ingathering at the year's end.
> [23]Three times in the year shall all your males appear before the Lord God, the God of Israel.
> ⇒ [24]For I will cast out the nations before you and enlarge your borders; neither shall any man desire [and molest] your land when you go up to appear before the Lord your God three times in the year.
>
> —Exodus 34:18, 22–24 (AMP)

Three feasts are mentioned here:

1. The *Feast of Unleavened Bread*
2. The *Feast of Weeks*
3. The *Feast of Ingathering*

In the Old Covenant with Jehovah the Hebrews were required to celebrate these three feasts each year. Still relevant to believers today, they are "types" of our faith experience, revealing a process of growth meant to be experienced by those in covenant with Him under the New Covenant. *The Feast of Unleavened Bread* is celebrated in conjunction with the Passover and marks a starting point of repentance. *The Feast of Weeks* and *the Feast of Ingathering* follow it. Both have to do with harvest and the bringing forth of fruit. The Feast of Weeks is referred to in Exodus 23:16 as the *Feast of Harvest* and is commonly called the "Day of Pentecost."

Table 1 lists the three feasts in blocks that include associated feasts that are also mandatory.

	*Table 1: Annual Hebrew Feasts* *Leviticus 23:4–44*
I	Passover
	Feast of Unleavened Bread
II	First Fruits
	Feast of Weeks (Feast of Harvest; Pentecost)
III	Feast of Trumpets
	Day of Atonement
	Feast of Ingathering (Feast of Tabernacles or Booths)

These feasts were significant to the individual and to the Hebrew people corporately. Likewise, as types, they are individually and corporately significant to Christians today.

The promised result of keeping all three feasts was victory over enemies and peace. While this is promised to all those newly born in Christ Jesus, realizing this (and other promises) in fullness is a process.

A great example of this principle is found in the life of Abraham. In Genesis, chapter 15, the Lord made a blood covenant with Abraham and promised this childless man that he would be the father of multitudes. He reiterated the promise to Abraham several times over the years and further promised him a son by his wife, Sarah, who was well along in years and barren. Struggling with confusion and unbelief, Abraham took matters into his own hands, producing Ishmael by his bondswoman, Hagar. Finally the Lord gave him the promised son from the womb of his wife. When the son had grown to be a young man, the Lord paradoxically commanded Abraham to sacrifice him as a burnt offering. But Abraham had faith that Jehovah would not allow him to kill his son, but would provide something else to sacrifice. He proceeded to obey God's command:

> [9]When they came to the place of which God had told him, Abraham built an altar there; then he laid the wood in order and bound Isaac his son and laid him on the altar on the wood.
> [10]And Abraham stretched forth his hand and took hold of the knife to slay his son.
> [11]But the Angel of the Lord called to him from heaven and said, Abraham, Abraham! He answered, Here I am.

¹²And He said, Do not lay your hand on the lad or do anything to him; for now I know that you fear *and* revere God, since you have not held back from Me *or* begrudged giving Me your son, your only son.
¹³Then Abraham looked up *and* glanced around, and behold, behind him was a ram caught in a thicket by his horns. And Abraham went and took the ram and offered it up for a burnt offering *and* an ascending sacrifice instead of his son!

—Genesis 22:9–13 (AMP)

It is very clear in verse twelve of this chapter that the Lord was testing Abraham in order to verify the quality of his faith. Abraham was no longer taking matters into his own hands. Obedience was not difficult now since his faith had grown so much. He knew that his faithful God would somehow do all that He had promised. At this point the promise became a "done deal" and Jehovah confirmed it by taking a solemn oath:

¹⁵The Angel of the Lord called to Abraham from heaven a second time

⇨ ¹⁶And said, I have sworn by Myself, says the Lord, that since you have done this and have not withheld [from Me] *or* begrudged [giving Me] your son, your only son,
¹⁷In blessing I will bless you and in multiplying I will multiply your descendants like the stars of the heavens and like the sand on the seashore. And your Seed (Heir) will possess the gate of His enemies,
¹⁸And in your Seed [Christ] shall all the nations of the earth be blessed *and* [by Him] bless themselves, because you have heard *and* obeyed My voice.

—Genesis 22:15–18 (AMP)

Abraham had been hoping in the promise for years, and Jehovah had reiterated the promise again and again. Still, it was not fulfilled. *Why?* In the above verses the Lord is not reiterating the promise; He is saying that the conditions required to see the promise fulfilled have now been met. Those conditions are *faith* and *obedience.* Jehovah would surely be faithful to the covenant He had made with Abraham, but an agreement or covenant *takes the actions of two.* In the covenant, Abraham had the immeasurable privilege of calling Jehovah his God. However, this privilege demands faith in and obedience to the commands of Jehovah. The same is true today! It is absurd for anyone to think that he or she may see the promises of God fulfilled without walking in faith and obedience. It is our responsibility in keeping *our* half of the deal. Faith is our part in the blood covenant with Jehovah that is sealed in the precious blood of Jesus Christ. This truth is discussed further in Hebrews 6:

[11]But we do [strongly and earnestly] desire for each of you to show the same diligence *and* sincerity [all the way through] in realizing *and* enjoying the full assurance *and* development of [your] hope until the end,

[12]In order that you may not grow disinterested *and* become [spiritual] sluggards, but imitators, behaving as do those who through faith (by their leaning of the entire personality on God in Christ in absolute trust and confidence in His power, wisdom, and goodness) and by practice of patient endurance *and* waiting are [now] inheriting the promises.

[13]For when God made [His] promise to Abraham, He swore by Himself, since He had no one greater by whom to swear,

¹⁴Saying, Blessing I certainly will bless you and multiplying I will multiply you.

⇨ ¹⁵And so it was that he [Abraham], having waited long *and* endured patiently, realized *and* obtained [in the birth of Isaac as a pledge of what was to come] what God had promised him.

¹⁶Men indeed swear by a greater [than themselves], and with them in all disputes the oath taken for confirmation is final [ending strife].

⇨ ¹⁷Accordingly God also, in His desire to show more convincingly *and* beyond doubt to those who were to inherit the promise the unchangeableness of His purpose *and* plan, intervened (mediated) with an oath.

⇨ ¹⁸This was so that, by two unchangeable things [His promise and His oath] in which it is impossible for God ever to prove false *or* deceive us, we who have fled [to Him] for refuge might have mighty indwelling strength *and* strong encouragement to grasp *and* hold fast the hope appointed for us *and* set before [us].

¹⁹[Now] we have this [hope] as a sure and steadfast anchor of the soul [it cannot slip and it cannot break down under whoever steps out upon it—a hope] that reaches farther *and* enters into [the very certainty of the Presence] within the veil,

²⁰Where Jesus has entered in for us [in advance], a Forerunner having become a High Priest forever after the order (with the rank) of Melchizedek.

—Hebrews 6:11–20 (AMP)

Suppose that on a Saturday morning a parent promises his or her children that in the evening they will get a pizza dinner and a trip to their favorite amusement park. Inherent in the promise is the knowledge that routine obedience is expected and routine Saturday chores must be completed. Bedrooms, yard leaves, and garage clutter all need to be cleaned up. If rebellion is encountered or if the chores are neglected, the trip may well be canceled. However, if chores are harmoniously completed the parent will finally say: "OK, kids, get in the car. We are leaving for the pizza parlor." This is like the Lord's oath. It's equivalent to saying, "You have met the requirements! It's a 'done deal.' Let's go!"

Another good example would be a person living in St. Louis, working for a large corporation there. The CEO has assured her that she will certainly have employment for the next fifteen years. She has announced her desire to work at other geographical locations. A year later she is assigned a job at a plant in New York City. She packs all of her goods and prepares to move. Deciding that she prefers the weather in San Diego to that in New York City, she moves to San Diego instead. A week after arriving in San Diego, she calls the CEO and complains that things are not working out for her. His response to her is, "What are you doing in San Diego? We don't even have a division there!"

Suppose that the Holy Spirit were her CEO. He might also tell her, "Why didn't you go where I told you to go? I had everything prepared for you! There was a job, a home, a church, with friendships all waiting for you there." We should not live like God has no plan and expect Him to bless ours. He does have a plan for running the universe and for establishing His Kingdom on this earth. We must cooperate with *His* plan if we want to be a part of what He is doing.

Our faith, cooperation, and obedience are absolutely critical to receiving the things that God has promised us. We must persevere in faith and obedience until we please the Father and

He says, "OK, I am convinced that the character-building I have been doing in this person is complete. It has been tested and confirmed. The fulfillment of the promise is now a 'done deal,' and surely it will come to pass."

CHAPTER 4

WATER BAPTISM AND UNLEAVENED BREAD

A blood sacrifice was required for the Hebrew people to be born as a nation that could rightfully call Jehovah their God. Abraham had stated in faith that the Lord would provide a lamb to be sacrificed as a substitute for Isaac. And God *did* provide a lamb (Genesis 22:13) that died in Isaac's place.

Isaac lived to give birth to Jacob (named *Israel* by God). Israel fathered twelve sons, whose descendents have been called the "Children of Israel." This great people came into being because of the substitutionary death of a lamb. The lamb died for them while they were yet merely unseen elements in Isaac's genetic makeup.

Israel's son Joseph and his eleven brothers became established in Egypt. Their descendents grew to be a great multitude of people and were forced into slavery under the Egyptians. After four hundred years of living in Egypt (Genesis 15:13, Exodus 12:40–41), the Lord Jehovah sent a deliverer named Moses to help them. He had just finished a forty-year period of testing

(Acts 7:30). Being approved by the Father, he was walking in the wisdom and power of Jehovah God. He was also displaying the fruit of a true servant of the Lord. Although he was manifesting incredible spiritual power, the Bible says that he was the meekest man on earth (Numbers 12:3).

The multitude of probably well-over-a-million people (Exodus 12:37–38) were waiting for the delivering power of God. Using Moses as His mouthpiece to admonish the Egyptians, the Lord repeatedly punished them and commanded them to free the Israelites. Then, enduring nine powerful, righteous judgments, the Pharaoh of Egypt refused to yield to the will of the Lord. The Hebrews remained slaves and their suffering even increased. Then the Lord issued the final blow that freed the Hebrews. He had Moses tell the people ahead of time what He was going to do.

> [12]For I will pass through the land of Egypt this night and will smite all the firstborn in the land of Egypt, both man and beast; and against all the gods of Egypt I will execute judgment [proving their helplessness]. I am the Lord.
> —Exodus 12:12 (AMP)

He also told the Israelites, through Moses, what to do in order to avoid being included with the victims. They were to kill a lamb and smear its blood above and on both sides of the door. When the Lord passed through to slay all the firstborn in the land, He would pass over the blood-marked homes without doing any harm. They were also given details for eating the lamb in a special meal with herbs and unleavened bread. The *bitter herbs* were to remind them of the misery of being enslaved in Egypt. Leaven is a symbol of corruption; they were to no longer have a diet of Egyptian corruption or any other corruption in their lives. They were to eat the meal *fully dressed* and ready for a journey. They were to eat the meal quickly, not slowly nor halfheartedly.

This meal, eaten before deliverance took place, is a very meaningful picture of the repentance required before being truly "saved" or born again through the blood of Jesus Christ. Recognizing the bitterness of sin and turning away from the corruption of it is prerequisite to being washed clean of sin and delivered from the power of the devil. The event of having the Lord pass over the Hebrew homes and the meal instituted to commemorate it was called the *Passover*. The Lord also commanded that Passover be observed annually (Exodus 34:18–25). The day that it was celebrated would be the first day of The Feast of Unleavened Bread.

> [15][In celebration of the Passover in future years] seven days shall you eat unleavened bread; even the first day you shall put away leaven [symbolic of corruption] out of your houses; for whoever eats leavened bread from the first day until the seventh day, that person shall be cut off from Israel.
> —Exodus 12:15 (AMP)

The two feasts taken together are referred to as The Feast of Unleavened Bread (not *The Passover)* in those scriptures stating that every male must come before the Lord three times each year (see Table 1, Chapter Three). This underscores the need for repentance when applying the blood. Being required to keep this feast for seven days following the application of the blood indicates that the effects of repentance are to be permanent.

WATER BAPTISM AND
UNLEAVENED BREAD

Living a holy life is to be continuous, seven days a week, not just a phenomenon for Sabbaths.

> ⁶[About the condition of your church] your boasting is not good [indeed, it is most unseemly and entirely out of place]. Do you not know that [just] a little leaven will ferment the whole lump [of dough]?
> ⁷Purge (clean out) the old leaven that you may be fresh (new) dough, still uncontaminated [as you are], for Christ, our Passover [Lamb], has been sacrificed.
> ⁸Therefore, let us keep the feast, not with old leaven, nor with leaven of vice *and* malice and wickedness, but with the unleavened [bread] of purity (nobility, honor) *and* sincerity and [unadulterated] truth.
>
> —1 Corinthians 5:6–8 (AMP)

When Abraham entered into covenant with Jehovah the Lord required that he be circumcised. This removal of a small bit of flesh symbolized his agreement to no longer be a servant of the flesh. In keeping with this covenant agreement, all male Hebrews were circumcised. This was another act of repentance prerequisite to eating the Passover meal and applying the blood on the doorposts for deliverance and protection.

> ⁴⁸When a stranger sojourning with you wishes to keep the Passover to the Lord, let all his males be circumcised, and then let him come near and keep it; and he shall be as one that is born in the land. But no uncircumcised person shall eat of it.
>
> —Exodus 12:48 (AMP)

Even under the Old Covenant Jehovah's love, deliverance, and protection were available to anyone willing to meet His simple conditions. One might ask, "Isn't God's love unconditional?" It most certainly is! He loves everyone and is, "not willing that any should perish." Our wonderful Creator is eager to enter into a love agreement with any willing person. In fact, Messiah Emmanuel *(God-come-in-the-flesh)* paid an excruciating price in order for every person to have such an opportunity. However, an agreement means that *two* people agree on something. In this case it means that a person agrees to resign from being a soldier in the devil's army and enlist in the army of the Lord. This means refusing to serve the flesh, sin, or anything other than the Lord Jesus Christ. This act, when accompanied with remorse for past offenses, is repentance.

> [9]The Lord does not delay *and* is not tardy *or* slow about what He promises, according to some people's conception of slowness, but He is longsuffering (extraordinarily patient) toward you, not desiring that any should perish, but that all should turn to repentance.
> —2 Peter 3:9 (AMP)

It was specified that the lamb sacrificed for Passover had to be completely healthy, with no unusual markings or deformities on him.

> [5]Your lamb *or* kid shall be without blemish, a male of the first year; you shall take it from the sheep or the goats.
> —Exodus 12:5 (AMP)

WATER BAPTISM AND
UNLEAVENED BREAD

After the priesthood was instituted for tabernacle worship, the priest would inspect the animals presented for sacrifice and reject any animal that was blemished. It was during preparation for the Passover that Jesus was delivered up to be crucified. At that same time, priests were examining animals presented for Passover sacrifice in order to verify their purity (John 19:14). Jesus, like a sacrificial animal, was presented to Caiaphas, the high priest, for examination. This same high priest had stated unwittingly earlier that Jesus should die in their behalf.

> [49]But one of them, Caiaphas, who was the high priest that year, declared, You know nothing at all!
> [50]Nor do you understand *or* reason out that it is expedient *and* better for your own welfare that one man should die on behalf of the people than that the whole nation should perish (be destroyed, ruined).
> [51]Now he did not say this simply of his own accord [he was not self-moved]; but being the high priest that year, he prophesied that Jesus was to die for the nation,
> [52]And not only for the nation but also for the purpose of uniting into one body the children of God who have been scattered far and wide.
>
> —John 11:49–52 (AMP)

Their frantic effort to recruit false witnesses was in itself ample admission that Jesus Christ was "without blemish." With this understanding, the high priests delivered Him up to be sacrificed. Thus He *became our Passover sacrifice* (1 Corinthians 5:7).

[57]But those who had seized Jesus took Him away to Caiaphas, the high priest, where the scribes and the elders had assembled.

—Matthew 26:57 (AMP)

[59]Now the chief priests and the whole council (the Sanhedrin) sought to get false witnesses to testify against Jesus, so that they might put Him to death;

—Matthew 26:59 (AMP)

[66]What do you think now? They answered, He deserves to be put to death.

—Matthew 26:66 (AMP)

As the Hebrews were commanded to eat the lamb with bitter herbs and unleavened bread, so the Lord commanded that we must eat His body and drink His blood if we are to have any part in Him and the work that He is doing.

[53]And Jesus said to them, I assure you, most solemnly I tell you, you cannot have any life in you unless you eat the flesh of the Son of Man and drink His blood [unless you appropriate His life and the saving merit of His blood].
[54]He who feeds on My flesh and drinks My blood has (possesses now) eternal life, and I will raise him up [from the dead] on the last day.
[55]For My flesh is true *and* genuine food, and My blood is true *and* genuine drink.
[56]He who feeds on My flesh and drinks My blood dwells continually in Me, and I [in like manner dwell continually] in him.

—John 6:53–56 (AMP)

WATER BAPTISM AND
UNLEAVENED BREAD

We are further admonished, as the Hebrews were, to celebrate a memorial meal. In it we humbly and gratefully remember the powerful sacrifice Christ made for our deliverance from the kingdom of darkness (Luke 22:19–20, 1 Corinthians 11:23–25).

In Egypt the Lord did exactly as He had warned. On the day following the Passover meal every Egyptian home had at least one dead person (Exodus 12:30). The Pharaoh finally yielded to the demands of Jehovah. The Hebrews were told that they could leave Egypt to make sacrifices of worship in the wilderness. The healing power of the covenant meal was also revealed. When this great multitude left Egypt, there wasn't one sick person among them (Psalm 105:37)!

As a loving Shepherd the Lord led the Hebrews out of Egypt. He manifested Himself to them as a *pillar of cloud* to lead them during the day. At night He was as a *pillar of fire* to give them light. He had them stop and camp next to the Red Sea. He intentionally placed them within striking distance of Pharaoh's army.

> ⁴ I will harden (make stubborn, strong) Pharaoh's heart, that he will pursue them, and I will gain honor *and* glory over Pharaoh and all his host, and the Egyptians shall know that I am the Lord. And they did so.
>
> —Exodus 14:4 (AMP)

Pharaoh pursued them, hoping to force their return to captivity. But the Lord parted the Red Sea, and the Hebrews fled from Pharaoh on a dry lakebed. They had a wall of water on both sides of them (Exodus 14:22). He put a cloud of darkness on Pharaoh's army but gave light to the Hebrews. As the army tried to pursue them on the dry lakebed, He sabotaged their chariots and closed the water on top of them. Not one Egyptian survived.

So, in going down into the Red Sea, the Hebrews were saved. It is most fitting that it was the Red Sea, for it speaks of the blood-cleansing of Jesus Christ in repentance and of water baptism. Egypt was not allowed to follow these believers into the new life. The sin and guilt that would have followed them was put to death, and they were not to return to its source. Their own walk through the sea symbolized that they were to consider themselves dead to Egypt and to their old lives. In this act they became one with Moses, who contained the purposes and plans of the Mighty Jehovah.

> [1]FOR I do not want you to be ignorant, brethren, that our forefathers were all under *and* protected by the cloud [in which God's Presence went before them], and every one of them passed safely through the [Red] Sea,
> [2]And each one of them [allowed himself also] to be baptized into Moses in the cloud and in the sea [they were thus brought under obligation to the law, to Moses, and to the covenant, consecrated and set apart to the service of God];
> —1 Corinthians 10:1–2 (AMP)

This is a very clear type of New Covenant repentance and baptism into Jesus Christ.

> [3]Are you ignorant of the fact that all of us who have been baptized into Christ Jesus were baptized into His death?
> [4]We were buried therefore with Him by the baptism into death, so that just as Christ was raised from the dead by the

glorious [power] of the Father, so we too might [habitually] live *and* behave in newness of life.

⁵For if we have become one with Him by sharing a death like His, we shall also be [one with Him in sharing] His resurrection [by a new life lived for God].

—Romans 6:3–5 (AMP)

¹⁰For by the death He died, He died to sin [ending His relation to it] once for all; and the life that He lives, He is living to God [in unbroken fellowship with Him].

¹¹Even so consider yourselves also dead to sin *and* your relation to it broken, but alive to God [living in unbroken fellowship with Him] in Christ Jesus.

—Romans 6:10–11 (AMP)

The Hebrews continued the first segment of the three-part journey. One of the stops was at a place called *Rephidim.* Here the multitude complained because there was no water for them to drink. The Lord instructed Moses:

⁶Behold, I will stand before you there on the rock at [Mount] Horeb; and you shall strike the rock, and water shall come out of it, that the people may drink. And Moses did so in the sight of the elders of Israel.

—Exodus 17:6 (AMP)

Now, in type, *Jesus* is the Rock, the One who sustained and provided for them in their travels. As He gave them water from a rock, so is He our Rock, giving us *living water.*

³And all [of them] ate the same spiritual (supernaturally given) food,
⁴And they all drank the same spiritual (supernaturally given) drink. For they drank from a spiritual Rock which followed them [produced by the sole power of God Himself without natural instrumentality], and the Rock was Christ.

—1 Corinthians 10:3–4 (AMP)

¹⁴But whoever takes a drink of the water that I will give him shall never, no never, be thirsty any more. But the water that I will give him shall become a spring of water welling up (flowing, bubbling) [continually] within him unto (into, for) eternal life.

—John 4:14 (AMP)

Even before the day of Pentecost the Lord Jesus gave the Holy Spirit to His followers. They received a well of water within their beings. This is not the same experience as the Baptism in the Holy Spirit, wherein a person is immersed in the Holy Spirit (Acts 1–2).

²¹Then Jesus said to them again, Peace to you! [Just] as the Father has sent Me forth, so I am sending you.
²²And having said this, He breathed on them and said to them, Receive the Holy Spirit!

—John 20:21–22 (AMP)

The ceremonial cleansing of a leper is another Old Covenant type, foreshadowing the cleansing of the new believer in Christ Jesus (Leviticus 14). The leper was first anointed with *blood* for cleansing. The priest then anointed him with *oil,* a symbol of the Holy Spirit that imparted Jehovah's presence, blessing, and empowerment in life. Before cleansing, the leper was not allowed in the camp of God's people. After cleansing, he was allowed in the camp and in the court of the tabernacle the same as any Hebrew, even one who is not a priestly Levite.

A new believer in Christ Jesus receives an impartation of faith and power in a measure unique to the individual. He receives the power to continue to seek the face of the Lord and to walk in the light that he is given. He must, however, choose to do so daily.

> [12]But to as many as did receive *and* welcome Him, He gave the authority (power, privilege, right) to become the children of God; that is, to those who believe in (adhere to, trust in, and rely on) His name—
>
> —John 1:12 (AMP)

> [6][So] if we say we are partakers together *and* enjoy fellowship with Him when we live *and* move *and* are walking about in darkness, we are [both] speaking falsely and do not live *and* practice the Truth [which the Gospel presents].
> [7]But if we [really] are living *and* walking in the Light, as He [Himself] is in the Light, we have [true, unbroken] fellowship with one another, and the blood of Jesus *Christ* His Son cleanses (removes) us from all sin *and* guilt [keeps us cleansed from sin in all its forms and manifestations].
>
> —1 John 1:6–7 (AMP)

CHAPTER 5

HOLY SPIRIT BAPTISM AND HARVEST

After a few stops in the wilderness Moses and the Hebrew people arrived at Mount Sinai. Moses went up to the mountain and Jehovah spoke to him out of it:

> ⁴You have seen what I did to the Egyptians, and how I bore you on eagles' wings and brought you to Myself.
> ⁵Now therefore, if you will obey My voice in truth and keep My covenant, then you shall be My own peculiar possession *and* treasure from among *and* above all peoples; for all the earth is Mine.
> ⁶And you shall be to Me a kingdom of priests, a holy nation [consecrated, set apart to the worship of God]. These are the words you shall speak to the Israelites.
>
> —Exodus 19:4–6 (AMP)

Jehovah reminded Moses of the miracles He had just done to save the Hebrews. He told him that as a people they could continue in this relationship with Him if they were obedient to His voice and kept His covenant. In doing so they would become priests.

Moses confronted the people with the offer; they agreed that they would do all that the Lord had spoken. When Moses returned with their answer, Jehovah told him to have the people cleanse themselves and come back on the third day.

> ^{16}The third morning there were thunders and lightnings, and a thick cloud upon the mountain, and a very loud trumpet blast, so that all the people in the camp trembled.
> ^{17}Then Moses brought the people from the camp to meet God, and they stood at the foot of the mountain.
> ^{18}Mount Sinai was wrapped in smoke, for the Lord descended upon it in fire; its smoke ascended like that of a furnace, and the whole mountain quaked greatly.
> ^{19}As the trumpet blast grew louder and louder, Moses spoke and God answered him with a voice.
> —Exodus 19:16–19 (AMP)

The ensuing events contain the basic defining elements of all the culture, politics, and religious life of the Hebrews. These elements are embodied in a decree of their covenant with the Mighty Jehovah. After warning the people not to come any closer to this divine encounter of Moses, Jehovah began His description of the agreement by giving him the "Ten Commandments." Many other rules of conduct, details of worship tabernacle construction, and requirements for worship followed these commandments. In fact, it was during this discourse between God and Moses that the requirement of three blocks of feasts was first mentioned.

¹⁴Three times in the year you shall keep a feast to Me.
¹⁵You shall keep the Feast of Unleavened Bread; seven days you shall eat unleavened bread as I commanded you, at the time appointed in the month of Abib, for in it you came out of Egypt. None shall appear before Me emptyhanded.
¹⁶Also you shall keep the Feast of Harvest [Pentecost], [acknowledging] the firstfruits of your toil, of what you sow in the field. And [third] you shall keep the Feast of Ingathering [Booths or Tabernacles] at the end of the year, when you gather in the fruit of your labors from the field.
¹⁷Three times in the year all your males shall appear before the Lord God.

—Exodus 23:14–17 (AMP)

While the exact day of the year for keeping the Feast of Pentecost was not yet given, Jewish tradition holds that Moses received The Ten Commandments on the Feast of Harvest, also called Pentecost.

The day originally set for the Feast of Harvest by Jehovah actually depended upon the time of occurrence of another feast, the Feast of First Fruits. The time of occurrence of the Feast of First Fruits depended in turn upon the time that the agricultural harvest began.

¹⁰Tell the Israelites, When you have come into the land I give you and reap its harvest, you shall bring the sheaf of the firstfruits of your harvest to the priest.
¹¹And he shall wave the sheaf before the Lord, that you may be accepted; on the next day after the Sabbath the priest shall wave it [before the Lord].

¹²You shall offer on the day when you wave the sheaf a male lamb a year old without blemish for a burnt offering to the Lord.

¹³Its cereal offering shall be two-tenths of an ephah of fine flour mixed with oil, an offering made by fire to the Lord for a sweet, pleasing, *and* satisfying fragrance; and the drink offering of it [to be poured out] shall be of wine, a fourth of a hin.

¹⁴And you shall eat neither bread nor parched grain nor green ears, until this same day when you have brought the offering of your God; it is a statute forever throughout your generations in all your houses.

—Leviticus 23:10–14 (AMP)

The Feast of Harvest occurred seven full weeks after the Feast of First Fruits.

¹⁵And you shall count from the day after the Sabbath, from the day that you brought the sheaf of the wave offering, seven Sabbaths; [seven full weeks] shall they be.

¹⁶Count fifty days to the day after the seventh Sabbath; then you shall present a cereal offering of new grain to the Lord.

¹⁷You shall bring from your dwellings two loaves of bread to be waved, made from two-tenths of an ephah of fine flour; they shall be baked with leaven, for firstfruits to the Lord.

—Leviticus 23:15–17 (AMP)

The Hebrews were always to be mindful that Jehovah was the Source of every blessing and every victory that they would experience. They were to walk continually in faith and gratitude that He would be faithful to His covenant with them and would provide accordingly. The Feast of First Fruits was to be an expression of these attitudes, exhibited in an act of worship. The very first of the ripened crop was presented to the priest. He would wave it before the Lord in thankful acknowledgment that Jehovah alone is the Provider. The priest would then present an offering of worship and thanksgiving to Him. Only then was it safe for them to partake of any of the harvest for themselves.

> [19]The first of the firstfruits of your ground you shall bring into the house of the Lord your God. You shall not boil a kid in its mother's milk.
>
> —Exodus 23:19 (AMP)

This is an important principle; it is mentioned twice in relation to first fruits (Exodus 34:26). Misuse of any of the blessings of the Lord can be harmful to those who received the blessings. Using His gifts to satisfy one's own lust, greed, or gluttony is using them to bring death, not life. He intends that all that He gives would be *life* to the recipient. The milk of a mother goat is intended to give life, not death, to her young. The intent of this commandment is to strongly impress that we are not to use the things that God intends for life as instruments of death. Just as the mother goat is to the kid, Jehovah is our only Source of life. He gives us all good things.

> [15]Then the evil desire, when it has conceived, gives birth to sin, and sin, when it is fully matured, brings forth death.
> [16]Do not be misled, my beloved brethren.
> [17]Every good gift and every perfect (free, large, full) gift is from above; it comes down from the Father of all [that gives] light, in [the shining of] Whom there can be no variation

[rising or setting] or shadow cast by His turning [as in an eclipse].

[18]And it was of His own [free] will that He gave us birth [as sons] by [His] Word of Truth, so that we should be a kind of firstfruits of His creatures [a sample of what He created to be consecrated to Himself].

—James 1:15–18 (AMP)

[3][Or] you do ask [God for them] and yet fail to receive, because you ask with wrong purpose and evil, selfish motives. Your intention is [when you get what you desire] to spend it in sensual pleasures.

—James 4:3 (AMP)

God wants to bless us with the abundance of His mighty provision. He will not give us things if we do not yet know how to use them in accordance with the principles of life. Nor will He give us anything that He knows will produce death instead of life.

[2]Beloved, I pray that you may prosper in every way and [that your body] may keep well, even as [I know] your soul keeps well *and* prospers.

—3 John 2 (AMP)

God puts first importance on the prosperity of our souls. Any other prosperity must be supportive of that. He sends other kinds of prosperity secondarily and only as they contribute to real spiritual growth, life, and love for Him. He sends other forms of prosperity as our souls prosper.

Jesus suffered, died, and arose from the dead so that we could receive His eternal life to live within us. He was producing new creatures: a crop of living human temples of Jehovah, having His law written on their hearts (Jeremiah 31:33). James 1:18 (previously quoted) states that the believers living at that time were first fruits of this crop, produced according to the will of Jesus Christ.

Exodus 23:19 (previously quoted) states that the first of the first fruits are to be presented to Jehovah. As Jesus Christ made atonement for sinful mankind, the first of the first fruits of His crop of new creations was waved before the Father.

> [50]And Jesus cried again with a loud voice and gave up His spirit.
> [51]And at once the curtain of the sanctuary of the temple was torn in two from top to bottom; the earth shook and the rocks were split.
> [52]The tombs were opened and many bodies of the saints who had fallen asleep in death were raised [to life];
> [53]And coming out of the tombs after His resurrection, they went into the holy city and appeared to many people.
> —Matthew 27:50–53 (AMP)

We must follow the shining example of our holy Master. The first fruits of all increase, whether material, social, or spiritual, belong to God.

> [3]To them also He showed Himself alive after His passion (His suffering in the garden and on the cross) by [a series of] many convincing demonstrations [unquestionable evidences and infallible proofs], appearing to them during forty days and talking [to them] about the things of the kingdom of God.

⁴And while being in their company *and* eating with them, He commanded them not to leave Jerusalem but to wait for what the Father had promised, Of which [He said] you have heard Me speak.

⇨ ⁵For John baptized with water, but not many days from now you shall be baptized with (placed in, introduced into) the Holy Spirit.

⁶So when they were assembled, they asked Him, Lord, is this the time when You will reestablish the kingdom *and* restore it to Israel?

⁷He said to them, It is not for you to become acquainted with *and* know what time brings [the things and events of time and their definite periods] or fixed years and seasons (their critical niche in time), which the Father has appointed (fixed and reserved) by His own choice *and* authority *and* personal power.

⇨ ⁸But you shall receive power (ability, efficiency, and might) when the Holy Spirit has come upon you, and you shall be My witnesses in Jerusalem and all Judea and Samaria and to the ends (the very bounds) of the earth.

—Acts 1:3–8 (AMP)

Fifty days after the Passover and the time when Jesus Christ waved the first of His first fruits before the Father, was the day of Pentecost, according to tradition. Before returning to the Father, He commanded the believers to wait in Jerusalem until they were empowered for service. Jerusalem was the seat of priestly service; it was the designated place for Hebrews to keep the feasts. At Mount Sinai Jehovah had covenanted with the Hebrews to make them a nation of priests. Now in Jerusalem those newly united to Jehovah in the New Covenant were being called to priestly service. They waited in the Upper Room, united in intercession.

Finally the day arrived. The Hebrews at Mount Sinai had been shaken by the power of the Mighty Jehovah. Soon they would feel His mighty power again!

> ¹⁶The third morning there were thunders and lightnings, and a thick cloud upon the mountain, and a very loud trumpet blast, so that all the people in the camp trembled.
> ¹⁷Then Moses brought the people from the camp to meet God, and they stood at the foot of the mountain.
> ¹⁸Mount Sinai was wrapped in smoke, for the Lord descended upon it in fire; its smoke ascended like that of a furnace, and the whole mountain quaked greatly.
> —Exodus 19:16–18 (AMP)

On this first Pentecost of the early Christian Church Jehovah God made himself known in similar manifestations.

> ¹AND WHEN the day of Pentecost had fully come, they were all assembled together in one place,
> ²When suddenly there came a sound from heaven like the rushing of a violent tempest blast, and it filled the whole house in which they were sitting.
> ³And there appeared to them tongues resembling fire, which were separated *and* distributed and which settled on each one of them.
> ⇨ ⁴And they were all filled (diffused throughout their souls) with the Holy Spirit and began to speak in other (different, foreign) languages (tongues), as the Spirit kept giving them clear *and* loud expression [in each tongue in appropriate words].
> —Acts 2:1–4 (AMP)

HOLY SPIRIT BAPTISM AND HARVEST

At the inauguration of the Old Covenant, Jehovah made Himself known in a loud trumpet blast, along with *smoke and fire* on the mountain. At the inauguration of the New Covenant, He came in a violent tempest blast; the people, not a mountain, were baptized or *immersed in the Holy Spirit* and tongues of fire sat upon them. Furthermore, He did not give them a set of rules on stone to obey; instead, He gave them the Holy Spirit, who would write the Law on their hearts.

> ¹⁴For by a single offering He has forever completely cleansed *and* perfected those who are consecrated *and* made holy.
> ¹⁵And also the Holy Spirit adds His testimony to us [in confirmation of this]. For having said,
> ¹⁶This is the agreement (testament, covenant) that I will set up *and* conclude with them after those days, says the Lord: I will imprint My laws upon their hearts, and I will inscribe them on their minds (on their inmost thoughts and understanding),
>
> —Hebrews 10:14–16 (AMP)

Under both covenants obedience to the voice of the Lord was required. Under the Old Covenant the Angel of the Lord was sent to guide them into the Promised Land.

> ²⁰Behold, I send an Angel before you to keep *and* guard you on the way and to bring you to the place I have prepared.
> ²¹Give heed to Him, listen to *and* obey His voice; be not rebellious before Him *or* provoke Him, for He will not pardon your transgression; for My Name is in Him.

^{22}But if you will indeed listen to and obey His voice and all that I speak, then I will be an enemy to your enemies and an adversary to your adversaries.

—Exodus 23:20–22 (AMP)

Under the New Covenant the Holy Spirit is given to guide us into sanctification, where the fullness of Christ is formed in us and His Law is written on our hearts. This is the greatest gift that we have from the Lord, and every other gift is given with this end goal in mind.

^{12}Now we have not received the spirit [that belongs to] the world, but the [Holy] Spirit Who is from God, [given to us] that we might realize *and* comprehend *and* appreciate the gifts [of divine favor and blessing so freely and lavishly] bestowed on us by God.

—1 Corinthians 2:12 (AMP)

The Lord Jesus Christ requires our utmost obedience to the Holy Spirit. The Hebrews (Exodus 23:21) were told that disobeying their guiding Angel was a transgression that would not be pardoned (see Appendix). Jesus Christ made it clear, likewise, that disrespect for the Holy Spirit will not be forgiven.

^{10}And everyone who makes a statement *or* speaks a word against the Son of Man, it will be forgiven him; but he who blasphemes against the Holy Spirit [that is, whoever intentionally comes short of the reverence due the Holy Spirit], it will not be forgiven him [for him there is no forgiveness].

—Luke 12:10 (AMP)

HOLY SPIRIT BAPTISM AND HARVEST

We are baptized in the Holy Spirit, immersed in Him, to receive empowerment for ministry and guidance into sanctification through the Word of God and the blood of Jesus Christ. Having His Law written on our hearts does not mean that we will have just an understanding of what He expects of us, for this understanding has been written on the human heart from the beginning. It means, that through the work of the Holy Spirit, our hearts will be changed to obey, as well as understand.

> [18]For God's [holy] wrath *and* indignation are revealed from heaven against all ungodliness and unrighteousness of men, who in their wickedness repress *and* hinder the truth *and* make it inoperative.
> [19]For that which is known about God is evident to them *and* made plain in their inner consciousness, because God [Himself] has shown it to them.
> [20]For ever since the creation of the world His invisible nature *and* attributes, that is, His eternal power and divinity, have been made intelligible *and* clearly discernible in *and* through the things that have been made (His handiworks). So [men] are without excuse [altogether without any defense or justification],
>
> —Romans 1:18–20 (AMP)

> [14]When Gentiles who have not the [divine] Law do instinctively what the law requires, they are a law to themselves, since they do not have the law.
> [15]They show that the essential requirements of the law are written in their hearts *and* are operating there, with which their consciences (sense of right and wrong) also bear witness; and their [moral] decisions (their arguments of reason, their

condemning or approving thoughts) will accuse or perhaps defend *and* excuse [them]

—Romans 2:14–15 (AMP)

Beginning with Adam and Eve, mankind has known that disobedience to the Creator is wrong and deserving of punishment. Enoch and Noah proved that it was possible to discern a path of obedience that is acceptable to Jehovah—and walk in it. Yet sin existed even before the laws given under the First Covenant were there to be violated. Mankind contained in the human soul and conscience the knowledge of what is right and wrong in the eyes of Jehovah. Violating that internal code for behavior was then, and still is, *sin.*

17So any person who knows what is right to do but does not do it, to him it is sin.

—James 4:17 (AMP)

Before the Law was given, mankind behaved as we see many behave today in a large organization where the individual has a great degree of freedom and responsibility to act according to what he or she knows is right. Often a few individuals violate their freedom and do things they know are wrong, even though there are no formal rules. When disciplined, their response may be, "I got in trouble, and I didn't even do anything wrong." Romans 1:20 says that evildoers are without excuse, even though they may plead ignorance.

To correct this problem in an organization, rules and guidelines are established that often restrict the freedom of everyone involved. This is done so that the *real offenders* can be pinned down, made to acknowledge their wrongdoing, and required to repent of their lawless behavior. Repentance is necessary for them to receive forgiveness and to function effectively with their managers and peers.

This is exactly what Jehovah did in instituting the Old Covenant as a preparatory measure for the New Covenant. Paul states that in the case of covetousness (Romans 7:7) the Law helped him to recognize sin. He praises the work of the Law, saying that it exposes sin:

> ^{12}The law therefore is holy, and [each] commandment is holy and just and good.
>
> ^{13}Did that which is good then prove fatal [bringing death] to me? Certainly not! It was sin, working death in me by using this good thing [as a weapon], in order that through the commandment sin might be shown up clearly to be sin, that the extreme malignity and immeasurable sinfulness of sin might plainly appear.
>
> —Romans 7:12–13 (AMP)

Paul continues this theme in his letter to the Galatians:

> ^{19}What then was the purpose of the law? It was added [later on, after the promise, to disclose and expose to men their guilt] because of transgressions *and* [to make men more conscious of the sinfulness] of sin; and it was intended to be in effect until the Seed (the Descendant, the Heir) should come, to *and* concerning Whom the promise had been made. And it [the law] was arranged *and* ordained *and* appointed through the instrumentality of angels [and was given] by the hand (in the person) of a go-between [Moses, an intermediary person between God and man].
>
> —Galatians 3:19 (AMP)

²⁴So that the law served [to us Jews] as our trainer [our guardian, our guide to Christ, to lead us] until Christ [came], that we might be justified (declared righteous, put in right standing with God) by *and* through faith.
²⁵But now that the faith has come, we are no longer under a trainer (the guardian of our childhood).

—Galatians 3:24–25 (AMP)

The Law is a schoolmaster that brings sinners to a place of repentance and faith in Jesus Christ. The Holy Spirit writes the Law of Jehovah on our hearts in a way far deeper than just an awareness of right and wrong. As Christ is formed in us, we become people who habitually live in the way that pleases Jehovah most.

In Exodus 29, Exodus 40, and Leviticus 8, Aaron and his sons were anointed for the priesthood and given the garments necessary to serve in the *Holy Place.* In the Baptism in the Holy Spirit, the believer is anointed for service and given gifts needed to worship God *in spirit and in truth,* to function in intercessory prayer, and to minister to the Body of Jesus Christ.

The gifts include 1) event manifestations of the Holy Spirit and, 2) vocational giftings for service. There are nine event manifestations of the Holy Spirit given in 1 Corinthians 12, which may be divided into three categories:

1) Revelation
    a) Word of Wisdom
    b) Word of Knowledge
    c) Discernment of Spirits

2) Power
   a) Faith
   b) Healing
   c) Miracles

3) Utterance
   a) Prophecy
   b) Tongues
   c) Interpretation of Tongues

Vocational gifts for serving the Body of Christ are mentioned in Ephesians 4, Romans 12, and 1 Corinthians 12. All of these *priestly gifts* are given to New Covenant believers for one reason—to help bring the Body of Christ to maturity:

> 12His intention was the perfecting *and* the full equipping of the saints (His consecrated people), [that they should do] the work of ministering toward building up Christ's body (the church),
> 13[That it might develop] until we all attain oneness in the faith and in the comprehension of the [full and accurate] knowledge of the Son of God, that [we might arrive] at really mature manhood (the completeness of personality which is nothing less than the standard height of Christ's own perfection), the measure of the stature of the fullness of the Christ *and* the completeness found in Him.
>
> —Ephesians 4:12–13 (AMP)

Evangelism is included in the process of bringing the Body of Christ to maturity. After the New Covenant priests were anointed and equipped on the Day of Pentecost, the resulting first fruits of new creatures were waved before the Lord, foretelling a massive harvest (Leviticus 23:15–17, previously quoted).

> [41]Therefore those who accepted *and* welcomed his message were baptized, and there were added that day about 3,000 souls.
> [42]And they steadfastly persevered, devoting themselves constantly to the instruction and fellowship of the apostles, to the breaking of bread [including the Lord's Supper] and prayers.
> [43]And a sense of awe (reverential fear) came upon every soul, and many wonders and signs were performed through the apostles (the special messengers).
>
> —Acts 2:41–43 (AMP)

CHAPTER 6

FIRE BAPTISM AND INGATHERING

It was mentioned in chapter four that the Lord sent Moses to be His appointed deliverer of the Hebrew people after he completed forty years in God's refinery. Forty years earlier, Moses had tried to begin the job in his own strength. He killed an abusive Egyptian taskmaster and had to flee from Egypt to save his own life (Exodus 2:12–15). He erred in beginning the job ahead of schedule and, in so doing, he had only his own strength to rely on.

Moses did not yet know how to cooperate with the power of God. He spent the next forty years working as a wilderness shepherd. All of this was preparatory training for his next job—a wilderness shepherd of the Hebrew people.

More than four hundred years earlier the Lord Jehovah had told Abraham He would bring powerful judgment on the nation enslaving his offspring (Genesis 15:13–14). The Lord had not forgotten His promise.

²⁴And God heard their sighing *and* groaning and [earnestly] remembered His covenant with Abraham, with Isaac, and with Jacob.

²⁵God saw the Israelites and took knowledge of them *and* concerned Himself about them [knowing all, understanding, remembering all].

—Exodus 2:24–25 (AMP)

Then the Lord spoke to Moses:

¹⁰Come now therefore, and I will send you to Pharaoh, that you may bring forth My people, the Israelites, out of Egypt.

¹¹And Moses said to God, Who am I, that I should go to Pharaoh and bring the Israelites out of Egypt?

—Exodus 3:10–11 (AMP)

Years before, Moses had felt the call of God on his life to do something for his people. Now, however, he was being sent. This is the biblical pattern! There is usually a time of preparation and testing between a person's initial calling and the time that he or she is actually sent to do the job.

David had already been anointed to be king, and yet he spent many years running for his life and hiding in caves before the prophetic anointing was fulfilled (1 Samuel 16:1–2 Samuel 2:4). Joseph had a prophetic dream of leadership. He spent many years in slavery and prison before becoming the second-most-powerful person in the Egyptian government. Like Abraham and the Hebrew people, he had his time of severe testing before entering into his personal Promised Land, appointed by God.

Many people receive a powerful and encouraging word from the Lord concerning their futures. When it does not come to pass in a week, they begin to lose hope and fear that they have been deceived. Then when their life circumstances begin to go in just the opposite direction of what they were promised, they *really* give up. Instead, they should be encouraged! Isn't this the biblical pattern? David was anointed to be king, but just the opposite happened—for a season! Joseph was promised a respected position of leadership, but just the opposite happened—for a season! Moses thought he was to deliver his beloved people, but just the opposite happened—for a season! Abraham was promised that he would be the father of multitudes, but just the opposite happened—for a season. When we receive a promise from the loving Father everything may go in reverse, but it is just for a season. It may be a long season, but still it is just a season.

He has given us a promise so that we will have something to hold on to that gives us hope while we go through a necessary time of pruning and character formation. We should thank Him for the promise and be faithful through the time of testing. Then we will see the promise fulfilled. But we must cooperate and allow Him to develop in us the character and fruits of the spirit appropriate to an ambassador of Jesus Christ.

The forty years that Moses spent in the wilderness as a shepherd yielded a change in his character. He had been hasty, not just in word but also in his actions, which resulted in an Egyptian's death. At that point there was not much hope of his being used by the Lord.

[20]Do you see a man who is hasty in his words? There is more hope for a [self-confident] fool than for him.

—Proverbs 29:20 (AMP)

When we walk in our own understanding, we have only our own strength to carry us and to apply against obstacles of the devil that block our way. The only way to bring God's power to bear in a situation is to connect with His mind and do it His way. When we do this, the flow of power is automatic. This power may initially manifest as a download of faith into the soul, confirming that we are on the right path and all is well. Across forty years, Moses was transformed from an assertive, self-confident person to one who would not go anywhere without the guarantee of God's support.

> [26]He who leans on, trusts in, *and* is confident of his own mind *and* heart is a [self-confident] fool, but he who walks in skillful *and* godly Wisdom shall be delivered.
> —Proverbs 28:26 (AMP)

The world that we live in today trains and conditions people to be just the opposite of what we need to be to work in unison with the Creator of the Universe. The power of humanity and the strength of the individual are deified. We are made to feel that we are as good as God—that we may function independantly, as powerful entities, the same as He does! However, there can be no sound mental health without an accurate self-image.

We need to understand that while God has called us to share His throne with Him for all eternity, this is an incredible act of mercy and benevolence. We certainly don't deserve it. He does a powerful miracle in transforming decrepit sinners into the image of Jesus Christ, also allowing us to share His throne. However, there is something that will never change: He is not a created being, and *we are!* We are the work of His Hand and we owe Him our respect, our obedience, and our humble worship!

The purpose of the third "annually required" appearance before the Lord is to strip us completely of all confidence in our own understanding and strength. It is a school of learning how to connect to *His* understanding and strength and trust Him alone. It is not an attitude that proclaims, "We can do pretty well on our own, but need His help to do our best." In fact, it is to agree with Him that without Him we can do *nothing*.

> ⁵ I am the Vine; you are the branches. Whoever lives in Me and I in him bears much (abundant) fruit. However, apart from Me [cut off from vital union with Me] you can do nothing.
>
> —John 15:5 (AMP)

A powerful lamp has the potential to produce a lot of light. That is what it was created to do. However, it has nothing to offer but darkness until it is plugged into an electrical power source. Likewise, the Lord has created us individually, with intended purposes and functioning. We cannot function correctly without being plugged into the *Holy Power Source.* To live consistently, we must stay plugged in without interruption. Jesus refers to this as *abiding.*

The "wilderness training school" instills in the believer a consistency in staying plugged into Holy Spirit power. Jesus said that this is how we will bear abundant fruit. Imagine a branch that is periodically disconnected from the vine before the season of harvest. If it produced any fruit at all that fruit would be stunted. Consistency is critical to results!

The Hebrews didn't see much fruit to eat as they wandered in the wilderness. Actually, they really did not have much of an "ingathering" at all until they entered the Promised Land. After they entered, they were to celebrate the Feast of Ingathering simultaneously with the Feast of Tabernacles or Booths. While taking joy in the blessings of a fruitful harvest they were to remember the time of testing when they dwelt in booths.

> [42]You shall dwell in booths (shelters) for seven days: All native Israelites shall dwell in booths,
> [43]That your generations may know that I made the Israelites dwell in booths when I brought them out of the land of Egypt. I am the Lord your God.
> —Leviticus 23:42–43 (AMP)

The booths they were commanded to live in were temporary huts made from leaf-covered tree branches (Leviticus 23:40–43). While celebrating a plentiful harvest they were to seriously remember that they did not always have it so good. They were to remember that their blessings were not automatic benefits. They were blessed only because Jehovah God was generous and merciful. Not only that, but there was an entire generation of Hebrews who died in the wilderness because of disobedience, murmuring, and refusing to develop a mature faith.

Corporately, the rebellious self-life had to die out before they could enter the Promised Land. Just as the self-life in Moses was put to death in the wilderness, so it was with the Hebrew nation. The purpose of this feast was to remind future generations that Jehovah made the Hebrews dwell in booths when He brought them out of Egypt. The "future generations" include New Covenant believers, who have been grafted into the offspring of Abraham through faith in Jesus Christ (Romans 11). We need to know that there is a time of endurance and testing before realizing fulfillment of the promises of God.

FIRE BAPTISM AND INGATHERING

At the baptism of Jesus, John the Baptist announced that this would be the case.

> [10]And already the ax is lying at the root of the trees; every tree therefore that does not bear good fruit is cut down and thrown into the fire.
> [11]I indeed baptize you in (with) water because of repentance [that is, because of your changing your minds for the better, heartily amending your ways, with abhorrence of your past sins]. But He Who is coming after me is mightier than I, Whose sandals I am not worthy *or* fit to take off *or* carry; He will baptize you with the Holy Spirit and with fire.
> [12]His winnowing fan (shovel, fork) is in His hand, and He will thoroughly clear out *and* clean His threshingfloor and gather *and* store His wheat in His barn, but the chaff He will burn up with fire that cannot be put out.
>
> —Matthew 3:10–12 (AMP)

Following the baptism in the Holy Spirit there would be a purification process, a burning away of chaff, individually and corporately. The promise of this refining and proving process was reconfirmed on the Day of Pentecost when the early church received power from heaven and tongues of fire were sitting on their heads. Zechariah also prophesied about this process.

> [9]And I will bring the third part through the fire, and will refine them as silver is refined and will test them as gold is tested. They will call on My name, and I will hear *and* answer them. I will say, It is My people; and they will say, The Lord is my God.
>
> —Zechariah 13:9 (AMP)

After promising the refining process, He also promises that prayers will be answered. This implies an increase in authority and power over the forces of evil. At this point the Lord also reaffirms to the people that He will be their God and they will be His people. The reason that prayers are answered is simple. God has a plan for bringing His Kingdom to fullness in the earth. In His infinite kindness and love He has chosen to share His authority with us and defeat the powers of darkness by the life of His Son living through us. Prayer is the avenue He has chosen for releasing His power on the earth in order to establish His Kingdom. That power is released as we pray according to His will. When we abide in Him, we act in accordance with the mind of Christ and we pray the will of Jehovah God.

> [7] If you live in Me [abide vitally united to Me] and My words remain in you *and* continue to live in your hearts, ask whatever you will, and it shall be done for you.
> [8] When you bear (produce) much fruit, My Father is honored *and* glorified, and you show *and* prove yourselves to be true followers of Mine.
> —John 15:7–8 (AMP)

When we stay plugged into the power source we speak His words. They are words of authority that speak His will into being. They are words that cause His Kingdom to come and His will to be done on earth as it is in Heaven. This will includes our manifesting the holiness and character of Jesus in the church. It also includes dispensing saving grace, deliverance, and healing power to the lost. All of this is fruit that honors and glorifies the Father. This produces a harvest and an *ingathering*.

When we abide we pray according to the Father's will.

¹⁴And this is the confidence (the assurance, the privilege of boldness) which we have in Him: [we are sure] that if we ask anything (make any request) according to His will (in agreement with His own plan), He listens to *and* hears us.
¹⁵And if (since) we [positively] know that He listens to us in whatever we ask, we also know [with settled and absolute knowledge] that we have [granted us as our present possessions] the requests made of Him.

—1 John 5:14–15 (AMP)

Prayer is not about establishing human intentions. The human being is to come into unison, agreement, with Jehovah God. Then, as God's intentions are established in the person's mind, the will of God is prayed and power is released.

¹⁸And the harvest of righteousness (of conformity to God's will in thought and deed) is [the fruit of the seed] sown in peace by those who work for *and* make peace [in themselves and in others, that peace which means concord, agreement, and harmony between individuals, with undisturbedness, in a peaceful mind free from fears and agitating passions and moral conflicts].
¹WHAT LEADS to strife (discord and feuds) *and* how do conflicts (quarrels and fightings) originate among you? Do they not arise from your sensual desires that are ever warring in your bodily members?
²You are jealous *and* covet [what others have] and your desires go unfulfilled; [so] you become murderers. [To hate is to murder as far as your hearts are concerned.] You burn with envy *and* anger and are not able to obtain [the gratification, the contentment, and the happiness that you seek], so you fight and war. You do not have, because you do not ask.

³[Or] you do ask [God for them] and yet fail to receive, because you ask with wrong purpose and evil, selfish motives. Your intention is [when you get what you desire] to spend it in sensual pleasures.

—James 3:18–4:3 (AMP)

The branch cannot fail to bring forth fruit according to the will of God when it abides continually with His life flowing through it. It will be great fruit! *How do we know?* The Lord Jesus Christ promised us that it would be (John 14:12). But we must complete the course of faith into the land to witness the fulfillment. What could have been more promising to the Hebrew people than a sample of the giant fruit in the land? Moses sent an advance party of spies into the Promised Land. They found giant enemies and opposition as well as giant fruit:

²³And they came to the Valley of Eshcol, and cut down from there a branch with one cluster of grapes, and they carried it on a pole between two [of them]; they brought also some pomegranates and figs.

—Numbers 13:23 (AMP)

²⁷They told Moses, We came to the land to which you sent us; surely it flows with milk and honey. This is its fruit.

—Numbers 13:27 (AMP)

³⁰Caleb quieted the people before Moses, and said, Let us go up at once and possess it; we are well able to conquer it.
³¹But his fellow scouts said, We are not able to go up against the people [of Canaan], for they are stronger than we are.

—Numbers 13:30–31 (AMP)

FIRE BAPTISM AND INGATHERING

In the land the spies saw such great fruit that it took two men to carry one cluster of grapes. Since leaving Egypt, two of the spies had grown in faith—enough to know that Jehovah God could do *anything*. Although they had all seen the same miracles, the other ten had failed to grow in the same way. They refused to put their trust completely in the Lord (Hebrews 3:7–13). Since they were still trusting in their own abilities, they limited their futures accordingly. It seems a person must be stripped of all confidence in self-ability before he or she will have a willingness to rely continuously on the Lord. Only then can we abide and draw continually on Jehovah's holy reservoir of power in order to win our battles.

All of those who rebelled and refused to trust God died in the wilderness without entering the Promised Land. Those few men of faith, and the new generation that entered the land with them, were great delights to the Lord.

> ³For they got not the land [of Canaan] in possession by their own sword, neither did their own arm save them; but Your right hand and Your arm and the light of Your countenance [did it], because You were favorable toward *and* did delight in them.
>
> —Psalm 44:3 (AMP)

He delighted in them because they believed Him and put their whole trust in Him. Without faith it is impossible to please Him (Hebrews 11:6). We are in covenant with Jehovah, through the blood of Jesus Christ, to obey the Holy Spirit. We have not been given a map showing us how to get to the Promised Land. We *have* been given a Guide and Counselor.

¹¹For what person perceives (knows and understands) what passes through a man's thoughts except the man's own spirit within him? Just so no one discerns (comes to know and comprehend) the thoughts of God except the Spirit of God. ¹²Now we have not received the spirit [that belongs to] the world, but the [Holy] Spirit Who is from God, [given to us] that we might realize *and* comprehend *and* appreciate the gifts [of divine favor and blessing so freely and lavishly] bestowed on us by God.

—1 Corinthians 2:11–12 (AMP)

We have a Bible that is filled with promises for us, but it is only when we follow our Guide that we will be able to discover their fulfillment. This might seem like a harsh statement, but without the Holy Spirit, the Bible is of no value at all! If we want to realize the fulfillment of the promises, we must have a Guide to take us into the Promised Land. He will enlighten our minds to comprehend the Word of God so that we will complete the journey. The book is of no value to any person who relies only on His own understanding.

⁶Now the mind of the flesh [which is sense and reason without the Holy Spirit] is death [death that comprises all the miseries arising from sin, both here and hereafter]. But the mind of the [Holy] Spirit is life and [soul] peace [both now and forever].

—Romans 8:6 (AMP)

It was mentioned earlier that in water baptism we are to *reckon ourselves dead* (Romans 6:11). There is a difference between that and the fulfillment of that reckoning as it is being discussed in this chapter. The difference that exists is the same as the difference between the sick person who is claiming "by His stripes I am healed," and another who is now getting up off of the sick bed. As we yield our obedience to the Holy Spirit, the death we have been confessing becomes a fulfilled promise. As we die to our own need to control and allow God's power to work in and through us, He has the room He needs to bring forth the fulfillment of other promises we have been claiming.

> [24]I assure you, most solemnly I tell you, Unless a grain of wheat falls into the earth and dies, it remains [just one grain; it never becomes more but lives] by itself alone. But if it dies, it produces many others *and* yields a rich harvest.
> [25]Anyone who loves his life loses it, but anyone who hates his life in this world will keep it to life eternal. [Whoever has no love for, no concern for, no regard for his life here on earth, but despises it, preserves his life forever and ever.]
> —John 12:24–25 (AMP)

When we walk faithfully with the Lord through difficulties our head knowledge is transformed into heart knowledge. Trusting Him in the depths of our inner man allows us to abide in Him with a simple, undistracted faith. As promised in Psalm 91, we will not be plagued by the fears that are so common to people. Instead, we are filled with the fullness of God, which includes the Presence of the Father.

> [17]May Christ through your faith [actually] dwell (settle down, abide, make His permanent home) in your hearts! May you be rooted deep in love *and* founded securely on love,

¹⁸That you may have the power *and* be strong to apprehend *and* grasp with all the saints [God's devoted people, the experience of that love] what is the breadth and length and height and depth [of it];

¹⁹[That you may really come] to know [practically, through experience for yourselves] the love of Christ, which far surpasses mere knowledge [without experience]; that you may be filled [through all your being] unto all the fullness of God [may have the richest measure of the divine Presence, and become a body wholly filled and flooded with God Himself]!

—Ephesians 3:17–19 (AMP)

Jesus promised that this would happen!

²³Jesus answered, If a person [really] loves Me, he will keep My word [obey My teaching]; and My Father will love him, and We will come to him and make Our home (abode, special dwelling place) with him.

—John 14:23 (AMP)

The intimate fellowship with the Father is foreshadowed in another Holy Day celebrated in the third block of feasts (Table 1, Chapter Three). It is the Day of Atonement (Leviticus 16:30). This is not just another way to celebrate the Passover and our deliverance from the kingdom of darkness. It signifies our access to intimate fellowship with the Father through the atoning blood of Jesus Christ.

The high priest was the only person allowed to perform the sacrifices on the Day of Atonement. In fact, it was the only day of the year that *anyone* was allowed to enter the Most Holy Place (also called the *Holy of Holies).*

The high priest first made atonement for himself and the other priests. He made a burnt offering of a ram and killed a young bull for a sin offering. He then took incense (representing a visible stream of prayer) and the blood of the bull into the Most Holy Place. He then covered the Mercy Seat with a cloud of incense and sprinkled the bull's blood on and in front it.

The incense represents the need for people to demonstrate an attitude of reverence and fear of the Lord by offering praise and worship before entering into His holy Presence. The priests were preparing to make atonement for the entire congregation, but first they had to make atonement for themselves. Only a blameless priest could act as a mediator for a sinful congregation. The sin offering would not be required by the blameless High Priest who would, at a future day, come to earth as the Mediator of a "better covenant." In the Passover Jesus was seen as the Sacrificial Lamb. On the Day of Atonement He is seen as the High Priest, as well.

> [20]And it was not without the taking of an oath [that Christ was made Priest],
>
> [21]For those who formerly became priests received their office without its being confirmed by the taking of an oath by God, but this One was designated *and* addressed *and* saluted with an oath, The Lord has sworn and will not regret it *or* change His mind, You are a Priest forever *according to the order of Melchizedek.*
>
> [22]In keeping with [the oath's greater strength and force], Jesus has become the Guarantee of a better (stronger) agreement [a more excellent and more advantageous covenant].
>
> —Hebrews 7:20–22 (AMP)

Here again we see the oath. The Mighty Messiah passed the test that no other man could pass. He was approved and sworn to be the High Priest forever. It is a "done deal" that can never be revoked. It is an entry into the Most Holy Place for those who believe on His Name and continue in faith and obedience. By so doing, we also inherit this promised fellowship with the Father.

At one moment Jesus was at the point of complete separation from the Father as He became one with the sin of all mankind. Scripture describes that moment:

> [46]And about the ninth hour (three o'clock) Jesus cried with a loud voice, Eli, Eli, lama sabachthani?—that is, My God, My God, why have You abandoned Me [leaving Me helpless, forsaking and failing Me in My need]?
>
> —Matthew 27:46 (AMP)

However, His shed blood and body were acceptable sacrifices to the Father. His atoning death provided forgiveness for our sins, and He immediately entered the Most Holy Place. The veil of the temple was torn in two to allow His entry!

> [50]And Jesus cried again with a loud voice and gave up His spirit.
> ⇒ [51]And at once the curtain of the sanctuary of the temple was torn in two from top to bottom; the earth shook and the rocks were split.
>
> —Matthew 27:50–51 (AMP)

We know that He did this so that we might follow after Him into the Presence of the Father. The promise is clear:

⇒ ¹⁹[Now] we have this [hope] as a sure and steadfast anchor of the soul [it cannot slip and it cannot break down under whoever steps out upon it—a hope] that reaches farther *and* enters into [the very certainty of the Presence] within the veil,

⇒ ²⁰Where Jesus has entered in for us [in advance], a Forerunner having become a High Priest forever after the order (with the rank) of Melchizedek.

—Hebrews 6:19–20 (AMP)

After the acting high priest made atonement for himself and the other priests, he offered atoning sacrifices for the rest of the congregation, for the Holy Place, for the Tent of Meeting, and for the altar: First he offered a ram as a *burnt offering*. Next he took two male goats and cast lots to see which of the two would be used as a *sin offering*. He then sacrificed the selected goat and took its blood into the Most Holy Place and sprinkled it on and in front of the Mercy Seat. According to procedures described in the Law, the altar was cleansed by the *sprinkling the blood* of the bull and the goat upon it.

The sin offerings and the sprinkling of blood were required to pay for man's sin and remove all guilt in the eyes of Jehovah God—a clear picture of Christ's atoning death.

¹³For if [the mere] sprinkling of unholy *and* defiled persons with blood of goats and bulls and with the ashes of a burnt heifer is sufficient for the purification of the body,

¹⁴How much more surely shall the blood of Christ, Who by virtue of [His] eternal Spirit [His own preexistent divine personality] has offered Himself as an unblemished sacrifice to God, purify our consciences from dead works *and* lifeless observances to serve the [ever] living God?

⇨ ¹⁵[Christ, the Messiah] is therefore the Negotiator *and* Mediator of an [entirely] new agreement (testament, covenant), so that those who are called *and* offered it may receive the fulfillment of the promised everlasting inheritance—since a death has taken place that rescues *and* delivers *and* redeems them from the transgressions committed under the [old] first agreement.

—Hebrews 9:13–15 (AMP)

⁴Because the blood of bulls and goats is powerless to take sins away.
⁵Hence, when He [Christ] entered into the world, He said, Sacrifices and offerings You have not desired, but instead You have made ready a body for Me [to offer];
⁶In burnt offerings and sin offerings You have taken no delight.
⁷Then I said, Behold, here I am, coming to do Your will, O God—[to fulfill] what is written of Me in the volume of the Book.
⁸When He said just before, You have neither desired, nor have You taken delight in sacrifices and offerings and burnt offerings and sin offerings—all of which are offered according to the law—
⁹He then went on to say, Behold, [here] I am, coming to do Your will. Thus He does away with *and* annuls the first (former) order [as a means of expiating sin] so that He might inaugurate *and* establish the second (latter) order.

—Hebrews 10:4–9 (AMP)

The high priest then utilized the second male goat to demonstrate another aspect of salvation not addressed in the first block of feasts (Unleavened Bread) in Table 1. The purpose of the *first* goat was to pay the sin debt owed in Jehovah God's holy system of justice. The *second* goat was for the purpose of removing the sting of guilt from the human memory. The high priest laid both of his hands on the head of the living goat and confessed the sins of the whole congregation of Israel over it. He thus transferred all of the sins of the people onto the goat. The goat was then taken into the wilderness and set free. It carried all of the iniquity of Israel to a land of forgetfulness so that the sins would be remembered no more (Leviticus 16:21–22). It is from this scripture that the term "scapegoat" originated. A *scapegoat* is one who takes the blame for the wrongdoing of another.

In the process of sanctification a believer realizes increasing victory over the sins that in the past have been besetting. As this happens, the bitter memory of the sin moves into the past. The forces of evil do not want the believer to experience the peace and joy of deliverance. The enemy will remind the believer of past failures with a flood of tormenting memories. We need to know that the salvation provided by our Lord Jesus Christ is complete, and being fully aware of it releases us from the painful memories!

Consider a man named John working on a computer in a corporate office setting. While performing some prohibited procedures he wipes out the system for the entire office. Without a doubt, the guilty party will be penalized for this error. The group supervisor tells John not to worry, saying that he will take full responsibility and all of the blame for this error. When confronted by the office manager, the supervisor tells her, "The computers are my responsibility, and I take full blame for all of the damage."

If, instead, he were to tell the manager, "John did a really stupid thing, but I am taking the blame for it," he would only be making a shallow pretense of being a scapegoat. In the atonement, the Mighty Lord Jesus Christ made such a complete sacrificial act that, in our identification with His act, He made it as though we had never sinned.

It has been said that "justified" means, "just as if I'd never sinned." Indeed, Jesus took the entire blame. Sin is not some mysterious substance that came into being through our act of disobedience and now needs to be destroyed. Sin is those very acts of disobedience, and our Jesus took those actions on Himself as His own responsibility.

> 21For our sake He made Christ [virtually] to be sin Who knew no sin, so that in *and* through Him we might become [endued with, viewed as being in, and examples of] the righteousness of God [what we ought to be, approved and acceptable and in right relationship with Him, by His goodness].
>
> —2 Corinthians 5:21 (AMP)

There is great victory in this. The evil one delights in putting a tormenting image of some long-past sin on the video screen of the believer's mind. Just add our Lord Jesus Christ to this image. He is standing about five feet away from you and is watching you commit the sin. He does not approve of what you are doing, but He is compassionate. He gently moves toward you until His body merges with yours. His body occupies the same space as yours while you continue your evil actions. Though Jesus Christ would never commit a sin, He is becoming one with your sinful actions. Now you unmerge from Him and back away until you are standing where He was to start with. He has changed places with you. He is now wearing your sinful actions, and you are free!!! When the devil comes accusing you can, with full knowledge of this exchange, say, "I didn't do it; He did!" That is what it means for One to be a scapegoat!

It must be made clear that this is for sin that has been confessed, repented of, cleansed by the blood of Christ, and overcome. It is our answer to an accusing devil—not an answer to a traffic cop, a court judge, or a spouse! This aspect of salvation is pictured on the Day of Atonement because it is for dealing with the memory of sin that has been repented of and overcome. It is for *confessed* sins, where deliverance has become a flesh and blood reality. Only then can the painful memory be removed. We are not to blame Jesus for evil actions that are continued behaviors.

We can go to Him for this same delivering comfort regarding the painful memories of foolish mistakes or shameful abuse. Sin is missing the mark, as in a foolish mistake, and Jesus came to bear our guilt and shame for this failure.

The Hebrew man who took the scapegoat into the wilderness washed his clothes and bathed before returning to camp. The bull and the goat used for the sin offerings were burned outside the camp. The man who burned them also washed his clothes and bathed before returning to camp, according to direction in the Law:

> ²⁷The bull and the goat for the sin offering, whose blood was brought in to make atonement in the Holy of Holies, shall be carried forth without the camp; their skins, their flesh, and their dung shall be burned with fire.
>
> —Leviticus 16:27 (AMP)

¹⁸And they began to salute Him, Hail (greetings, good health to You, long life to You), King of the Jews!
¹⁹And they struck His head with a staff made of a [bamboo-like] reed and spat on Him and kept bowing their knees in homage to Him.
²⁰And when they had [finished] making sport of Him, they took the purple [robe] off of Him and put His own clothes on Him. And they led Him out [of the city] to crucify Him.

—Mark 15:18–20 (AMP)

¹¹For when the blood of animals is brought into the sanctuary by the high priest as a sacrifice for sin, the victims' bodies are burned outside the limits of the camp.
¹²Therefore Jesus also suffered *and* died outside the [city's] gate in order that He might purify *and* consecrate the people through [the shedding of] His own blood *and* set them apart as holy [for God].
¹³Let us then go forth [from all that would prevent us] to Him outside the camp [at Calvary], bearing the contempt *and* abuse *and* shame with Him.

—Hebrews 13:11–13 (AMP)

We have an incredible and powerful Salvation—"so great a Salvation" (Hebrews 2:3) indeed! The more we understand about it, the more overwhelming our joy will become. Celebrating this great joy is one intention of the Feast of Trumpets (also a Block 3 feast, Table 1).

¹ON THE first day of the seventh month [on New Year's Day of the civil year], you shall have a holy [summoned] assembly; you shall do no servile work. It is a day of blowing of trumpets for you [everyone blowing who wishes, proclaiming that the

glad New Year has come and that the great Day of Atonement and the Feast of Tabernacles are now approaching].

—Numbers 29:1 (AMP)

We are warned repeatedly not to play games with God! He has taken our desperate need seriously, and He expects us to do the same. He paid the full, infinite price for our salvation. He has given us everything that we need to complete the course, and this includes the guidance and comfort of the Holy Spirit. The only thing that can keep a believer from finishing the race is "an evil heart of unbelief" (King James Version).

^{12}[Therefore beware] brethren, take care, lest there be in any one of you a wicked, unbelieving heart [which refuses to cleave to, trust in, and rely on Him], leading you to turn away *and* desert *or* stand aloof from the living God.

^{13}But instead warn (admonish, urge, and encourage) one another every day, as long as it is called Today, that none of you may be hardened [into settled rebellion] by the deceitfulness of sin [by the fraudulence, the stratagem, the trickery which the delusive glamour of his sin may play on him].

^{14}For we have become fellows with Christ (the Messiah) *and* share in all He has for us, if only we hold our first newborn confidence *and* original assured expectation [in virtue of which we are believers] firm *and* unshaken to the end.

^{15}Then while it is [still] called Today, if you would hear His voice *and* when you hear it, do not harden your hearts as in the rebellion [in the desert, when the people provoked and irritated and embittered God against them].

^{16}For who were they who heard *and* yet were rebellious *and* provoked [Him]? Was it not all those who came out of Egypt led by Moses?

¹⁷And with whom was He irritated *and* provoked *and* grieved for forty years? Was it not with those who sinned, whose dismembered bodies were strewn *and* left in the desert?
¹⁸And to whom did He swear that they should not enter His rest, but to those who disobeyed [who had not listened to His word and who refused to be compliant or be persuaded]?
—Hebrews 3:12–18 (AMP)

The rest that was offered to the Hebrews was the Promised Land—a place of fruitfulness and massive ingathering. For us it is a place of abiding in Christ and in the power flow of the Holy Spirit. In this abiding His fruit will appear on us, for we are *the branches.* It is not a place of weariness of labor, because His Spirit flows through us to accomplish His work according to His will. All we have to do is be willing, obedient, and walking in the faith that He will do all that He has promised. We must be willing to cease from our own agenda and die to our own plan. We are admonished to enter this rest because it is the will of God for us.

¹⁰For he who has once entered [God's] rest also has ceased from [the weariness and pain] of human labors, just as God rested from those labors peculiarly His own.
¹¹Let us therefore be zealous *and* exert ourselves *and* strive diligently to enter that rest [of God, to know and experience it for ourselves], that no one may fall *or* perish by the same kind of unbelief *and* disobedience [into which those in the wilderness fell].
—Hebrews 4:10–12 (AMP)

Ceasing from our own work does not mean that we are left motionless with nothing to do. He prepared good works for us to walk in before the foundation of the world. All we have to do is allow the Holy Spirit to flow through us to accomplish the works that He has *already prepared.*

> [10]For we are God's [own] handiwork (His workmanship), recreated in Christ Jesus, [born anew] that we may do those good works which God predestined (planned beforehand) for us [taking paths which He prepared ahead of time], that we should walk in them [living the good life which He prearranged and made ready for us to live].
>
> —Ephesians 2:10 (AMP)

When we get up in the morning we should get up looking for the outlined footprints on the floor and on the ground, showing us where to step in order to walk in all of the great and wonderful works God planned for us before the foundation of the world. It is *a rest* in yielding to His plan for the universe.

> [11]Therefore, remember that at one time you were Gentiles (heathens) in the flesh, called Uncircumcision by those who called themselves Circumcision, [itself a mere mark] in the flesh made by human hands.
>
> —Ephesians 2:11 (AMP)

Under the Old Covenant, circumcision of all Hebrew males was required. Under the New Covenant, God is not concerned with a physical operation on the male. He requires a "trimmed," changed heart in every believer.

> [11]In Him also you were circumcised with a circumcision not made with hands, but in a [spiritual] circumcision [performed

by] Christ by stripping off the body of the flesh (the whole corrupt, carnal nature with its passions and lusts).

¹²[Thus you were circumcised when] you were buried with Him in [your] baptism, in which you were also raised with Him [to a new life] through [your] faith in the working of God [as displayed] when He raised Him up from the dead.

—Colossians 2:11–12 (AMP)

³For we [Christians] are the true circumcision, who worship God in spirit *and* by the Spirit of God and exult *and* glory *and* pride ourselves in Jesus Christ, and put no confidence *or* dependence [on what we are] in the flesh *and* on outward privileges *and* physical advantages *and* external appearances—

—Philippians 3:3 (AMP)

Jeremiah expressed the profound sorrow of Jehovah God frequently as he wept over the Hebrews' unfaithfulness to Him. He prophesied that there would be a New Covenant with the Hebrews, wherein their evil hearts would be changed:

³¹Behold, the days are coming, says the Lord, when I will make a new covenant with the house of Israel and with the house of Judah,

³²Not according to the covenant which I made with their fathers in the day when I took them by the hand to bring them out of the land of Egypt, My covenant which they broke, although I was their Husband, says the Lord.

³³But this is the covenant which I will make with the house of Israel: After those days, says the Lord, I will put My law within them, and on their hearts will I write it; and I will be their God, and they will be My people.

—Jeremiah 31:31–33 (AMP)

FIRE BAPTISM AND INGATHERING

Under the Old Covenant, the Lord wrote His commandments on stone. Obedience to these commandments was essential to being one of His people. Under the New Covenant, we have been given the Holy Spirit to obey. As we do so, He writes His commandments on our hearts.

> [14]For by a single offering He has forever completely cleansed *and* perfected those who are consecrated *and* made holy.
> [15]And also the Holy Spirit adds His testimony to us [in confirmation of this]. For having said,
> [16]This is the agreement (testament, covenant) that I will set up *and* conclude with them after those days, says the Lord: I will imprint My laws upon their hearts, and I will inscribe them on their minds (on their inmost thoughts and understanding),
> —Hebrews 10:14–16 (AMP)

One more facet of the third appearance before God is that of overcoming. We overcome sin by obedient endurance and dying to our self-determination.

> [1]SO, SINCE Christ suffered in the flesh for us, for you, arm yourselves with the same thought and purpose [patiently to suffer rather than fail to please God]. For whoever has suffered in the flesh [having the mind of Christ] is done with [intentional] sin [has stopped pleasing himself and the world, and pleases God],
> [2]So that he can no longer spend the rest of his natural life living by [his] human appetites and desires, but [he lives] for what God wills.
> —1 Peter 4:1–2 (AMP)

This sanctification cannot occur apart from the powerful work of the blood of Jesus Christ. Of this we testify:

> [11]And they have overcome (conquered) him by means of the blood of the Lamb and by the utterance of their testimony, for they did not love *and* cling to life even when faced with death [holding their lives cheap till they had to die for their witnessing].
>
> —Revelation 12:11 (AMP)

When we present our bodies as living sacrifices to God (Romans 12:1–2) we obey Him and die to our own desires. Whether or not this leads immediately to physical death is purely His choice. Our willingness of heart is what He wants to see.

Wonderful promises to those who overcome are abundantly listed in a series of addresses to the seven churches (Revelation 2–3). Among these is the promise of kingship:

> [26]And he who overcomes (is victorious) and who obeys My commands to the [very] end [doing the works that please Me], I will give him authority *and* power over the nations;
> [27]And he shall rule them with a sceptre (rod) of iron, as when earthen pots are broken in pieces, and [his power over them shall be] like that which I Myself have received from My Father;
>
> —Revelation 2:26–27 (AMP)

This anointing of power and authority is foreshadowed in the Old Testament kings of Israel and Judah. Through the anointing with oil by prophet and/or priest, men received the sanction and backing of Jehovah God to function in this office of leadership. A large number of saints (144,000) are pictured with Christ in Revelation 14:

> [1]THEN I looked, and behold, the Lamb stood on Mount Zion, and with Him 144,000 [men] who had His name and His Father's name inscribed on their foreheads.
>
> —Revelation 14:1 (AMP)

Here they are seen as a group standing with the King of Kings on Mount Zion. Mount Zion, sometimes called the "City of David," was then the seat of kingly leadership and authority.

> [7]Nevertheless, David took the stronghold of Zion; that is, the City of David.
>
> —2 Samuel 5:7 (AMP)

> [2]Fair *and* beautiful in elevation, is the joy of all the earth— Mount Zion [the City of David], to the northern side [Mount Moriah and the temple], the [whole] city of the Great King!
>
> —Psalm 48:2 (AMP)

> [11]For to you is born this day in the town of David a Savior, Who is Christ (the Messiah) the Lord!
>
> —Luke 2:11 (AMP)

The same numbers of saints are mentioned in Revelation 7:4. In both chapter 7 and chapter 14 they are described as being *specially marked by God* because of their holiness. They have remained faithful and endured an incredible time of purification and testing. Their sanctification is a flesh and blood reality, and kingship has been conferred to them. They are standing on Mount Zion, the City of Kings, with King Jesus Christ.

Historically, there have been events of major importance to the corporate church that were concurrent with the first two mandatory blocks of feasts. It seems reasonable to expect that the Lord will honor the third block of feasts (Table 1) in the same way. It will be a corporate appearance of the church in the Most Holy Place with the Holy Father. Only the Father knows the exact day and hour that this gigantic heavenly Feast of Ingathering will take place (Acts 1:7).

> [32]But of that day or that hour not a [single] person knows, not even the angels in heaven, nor the Son, but only the Father.
> —Mark 13:32 (AMP)

It was with this event in mind that God created the universe. Being prepared for it is worth any sacrifice that may be required. What a privilege it will be to stand with Jesus where He is seated at the right Hand of the Father!

> [36]Keep awake then *and* watch at all times [be discreet, attentive, and ready], praying that you may have the full strength *and* ability *and* be accounted worthy to escape all these things [taken together] that will take place, and to stand in the presence of the Son of Man.
> —Luke 21:36 (AMP)

> [7]He who is victorious shall inherit all these things, and I will be God to him and he shall be My son.
> [8]But as for the cowards *and* the ignoble *and* the contemptible *and* the cravenly lacking in courage *and* the cowardly

submissive, and as for the unbelieving and faithless, and as for the depraved and defiled with abominations, and as for murderers and the lewd *and* adulterous and the practicers of magic arts and the idolaters (those who give supreme devotion to anyone or anything other than God) and all liars (those who knowingly convey untruth by word or deed)—[all of these shall have] their part in the lake that blazes with fire and brimstone. This is the second death.

—Revelation 21:7–8 (AMP)

Table 2: Old and New Blood Covenant Differences		
Covenant	Old	New
Priest(s)	Aaron and Sons	Son of God
Sacrificial Blood	Animal	Son of God
Sacrificial Body	Animal	Son of God
Obey	Law	Holy Spirit
Tablet	Stone	The Heart
Circumcision	Flesh	The Heart
Sacrifice	Annually	Once Only

Table 3: Comparative Aspects of Baptisms and Feasts			
Baptism or Feast	Water or Unleavened Bread	Holy Spirit or Harvest	Fire or Ingathering
Purpose	Repentance, Cleansing, and Salvation	Empower for Service and Endurance	Sanctification, Proving, and Authority
Godhead Emphasis	Son	Holy Spirit	Father
Anointing	Lepers'	Priests'	Kings'
Journey	Depart World or Egypt	Receive Power and Direction	Enter Promised Land
Life Process	Born of the Spirit	Walk and Talk in the Spirit	Abide in Christ
Temple Process	Receive Christ and Holy Spirit	Immersed in Holy Spirit	Filled with Fullness of God
Tabernacle Similitude	Tabernacle Court	Holy Place	Most Holy Place
New Kingdom Correlation	New Earth	New Jerusalem	New Mount Zion
Service	Zealous in Human Strength	Yielding to Holy Spirit	Have Entered His Rest

CHAPTER 7

GOD SIGNS

So, what is the end of the matter? What does God want, and where have all the signs been leading to for me and you? The end of the matter is this: To die to your own will and thus be fully equipped for service. To enter into His rest by letting His life live in you and empower you for everything that He calls you to do. This is entering the land of milk and honey and celebrating a powerful ingathering of fruit.

> 15Blessed (happy, fortunate, to be envied) are the people who know the joyful sound [who understand and appreciate the spiritual blessings symbolized by the feasts]; they walk, O Lord, in the light *and* favor of Your countenance!
> 16In Your name they rejoice all the day, and in Your righteousness they are exalted.
> 17For You are the glory of their strength [their proud adornment], and by Your favor our horn is exalted *and* we walk with uplifted faces!
>
> —Psalm 89:15–17 (AMP)

This *place of rest* includes full sanctification through the atonement. As you become a body filled and flooded with the Holy Triune Creator, there will be no room for sickness in your body. Being one with the Living Word, the Word will become flesh in your being. You will be a "living epistle."

This is a wonderful and mighty inheritance—and it becomes a reality for those who commit to trust the Savior fully, regardless of the price. Only God Himself knows the unique plan for your personal growth schedule. Only He knows just how He wants to shape you to take your place in His heavenly structure for eternity. Only He knows the plan for the remainder of your life.

> [11]In Him we also were made [God's] heritage (portion) and we obtained an inheritance; for we had been foreordained (chosen and appointed beforehand) in accordance with His purpose, Who works out everything in agreement with the counsel and design of His [own] will,
>
> —Ephesians 1:11 (AMP)

As Jesus was preparing to return to the Father He promised that He would not leave us alone. He said that He would send a "Comforter" to be our friend and guide. Since Pentecost, the tender and loving Holy Spirit has been here to guide us into receiving our blood-bought inheritance. Just as He convicted us of sin and drew us to Jesus Christ, so He will lead us into the complete fulfillment of our Savior's promises. He is here to glorify the name of Jesus Christ, and He responds powerfully when people pay proper respect to that name. He is Christ's voice here on earth, and He gives meaning to the written Word of God. It is necessary that we *know* His voice and obey it.

27The sheep that are My own hear *and* are listening to My voice; and I know them, and they follow Me.

—John 10:27 (AMP)

No two people have identical relationships or "walks" with God. He also has a unique place for each person in eternity. The required preparation processes may vary widely. The suffering appointed to one individual may differ immensely from that of another. We all have one common requirement: obedience to the Holy Spirit! We must know His voice and pay attention to His step by step instructions.

21And your ears will hear a word behind you, saying, This is the way; walk in it, when you turn to the right hand and when you turn to the left.

—Isaiah 30:21 (AMP)

8I [the Lord] will instruct you and teach you in the way you should go; I will counsel you with My eye upon you.

—Psalm 32:8 (AMP)

The Bible is the record of man's fall from being in communion with Jehovah God to a place of decrepit suffering—and of God's plan to restore the human race to a place of communion with Himself. Knowing Him is life, and He wants to bring us into a fulfilling relationship with Himself. Any spiritual endeavor that does not have this as the end purpose is just lifeless religion.

10[For my determined purpose is] that I may know Him [that I may progressively become more deeply and intimately acquainted with Him, perceiving and recognizing and understanding the wonders of His Person more strongly and

more clearly], and that I may in that same way come to know
the power outflowing from His resurrection [which it exerts
over believers], and that I may so share His sufferings as to
be continually transformed [in spirit into His likeness even]
to His death, [in the hope]

¹¹That if possible I may attain to the [spiritual and moral]
resurrection [that lifts me] out from among the dead [even
while in the body].

¹²Not that I have now attained [this ideal], or have already
been made perfect, but I press on to lay hold of (grasp) *and*
make my own, that for which Christ Jesus (the Messiah) has
laid hold of me *and* made me His own.

—Philippians 3:10–12 (AMP)

Jesus Himself made it clear that just knowing the Scriptures
is not enough. We must know *Him*. A person who reads a lot
of an author's material may feel like he knows him. There is,
however, a great difference between that and actually meeting
the author.

³⁹You search *and* investigate *and* pore over the Scriptures
diligently, because you suppose *and* trust that you have
eternal life through them. And these [very Scriptures] testify
about Me!

—John 5:39 (AMP)

Abundance of study, attendance at meetings, and faithful
service masquerade as a destination in our search for purpose,
but there is no substitute for knowing Him!

He will speak to us individually in ways that He chooses, not
in the ways that we may request or demand. As the Holy Spirit

enlightens our minds to the truths of God's Word, He may speak to us through our everyday circumstances, through the words of others, in devotional readings or occurrences in nature, in dreams, visions, a still small voice within, or any combination of these. Although it is rare, He may even speak in an audible voice. He may be very tender and subtle, or He may be stern and blunt, according to His purposes and our need.

In teaching certain principles that He wants us to operate by, He may give *line upon line* over long periods of time. We must read His Scripture and the signposts that He puts in our lives. This is not to demand signs and proofs as an evil generation does (Luke 11:29). It is to pay attention to the many ways that the Holy Spirit is trying to talk to us.

Remember that His only goal is to help you receive your blood-bought promises so that Christ is glorified. He is waiting and watching for your full cooperation. Will you be attentive to His voice? Can you resist such a loving Comforter, Who always has your best interest at heart? He wants to help you avoid the pitfalls of evil! Will you hear His voice and heed the warning signs that He posts in your life? He has a path charted for the rest of your life, which He planned before He created the universe. It may not be an easy one, but it is the center of His will! Are you willing to let Him guide you in every detail of your life and stay on that path?

> 26For what will it profit a man if he gains the whole world and forfeits his life [his blessed life in the kingdom of God]? Or what would a man give as an exchange for his [blessed] life [in the kingdom of God]?
>
> —Matthew 16:26 (AMP)

If you are willing to do whatever it takes to finish the course with Him, tell Him so now! And start watching for the *God signs* all along the highway that leads to eternity.

APPENDIX : IS OBEDIENCE OPTIONAL?

The best answer to this question can be found in the following key scriptures:

²⁵Not forsaking or neglecting to assemble together [as believers], as is the habit of some people, but admonishing (warning, urging, and encouraging) one another, and all the more faithfully as you see the day approaching.

²⁶For if we go on deliberately and willfully sinning after once acquiring the knowledge of the Truth, there is no longer any sacrifice left to atone for [our] sins [no further offering to which to look forward].

²⁷[There is nothing left for us then] but a kind of awful and fearful prospect and expectation of divine judgment and the fury of burning wrath and indignation which will consume those who put themselves in opposition [to God].

²⁸Any person who has violated and [thus] rejected and set at naught the Law of Moses is put to death without pity or mercy on the evidence of two or three witnesses.

²⁹How much worse (sterner and heavier) punishment do you suppose he will be judged to deserve who has spurned and [thus] trampled underfoot the Son of God, and who has considered the covenant blood by which he was consecrated common and unhallowed, thus profaning it and insulting and outraging the [Holy] Spirit [Who imparts] grace (the unmerited favor and blessing of God)?

³⁰For we know Him Who said, Vengeance is Mine [retribution and the meting out of full justice rests with Me]; I will repay [I will exact the compensation], says the Lord. And again, The Lord will judge and determine and solve and settle the cause and the cases of His people.

³¹It is a fearful (formidable and terrible) thing to incur the divine penalties and be cast into the hands of the living God!

—Hebrews 10:25–31 (AMP)

²⁰That is true. But they were broken (pruned) off because of their unbelief (their lack of real faith), and you are established through faith [because you do believe]. So do not become proud and conceited, but rather stand in awe and be reverently afraid.

²¹For if God did not spare the natural branches [because of unbelief], neither will He spare you [if you are guilty of the same offense].

²²Then note and appreciate the gracious kindness and the severity of God: severity toward those who have fallen, but God's gracious kindness to you—provided you continue in His grace and abide in His kindness; otherwise you too will be cut off (pruned away).

—Romans 11:20–22 (AMP)

[5]Now I want to remind you, though you were fully informed once for all, that though the Lord [at one time] delivered a people out of the land of Egypt, He subsequently destroyed those [of them] who did not believe [who refused to adhere to, trust in, and rely upon Him].

[6]And angels who did not keep (care for, guard, and hold to) their own first place of power but abandoned their proper dwelling place—these He has reserved in custody in eternal chains (bonds) under the thick gloom of utter darkness until the judgment and doom of the great day.

[7][The wicked are sentenced to suffer] just as Sodom and Gomorrah and the adjacent towns—which likewise gave themselves over to impurity and indulged in unnatural vice and sensual perversity—are laid out [in plain sight] as an exhibit of perpetual punishment [to warn] of everlasting fire.

—Jude 5–7 (AMP)

[20]For if, after they have escaped the pollutions of the world through [the full, personal] knowledge of our Lord and Savior Jesus Christ, they again become entangled in them and are overcome, their last condition is worse [for them] than the first.

[21]For never to have obtained a [full, personal] knowledge of the way of righteousness would have been better for them than, having obtained [such knowledge], to turn back from the holy commandment which was [verbally] delivered to them.

[22]There has befallen them the thing spoken of in the true proverb, The dog turns back to his own vomit, and, The sow is washed only to wallow again in the mire.

—2 Peter 2:20–22 (AMP)

⁴For it is impossible [to restore and bring again to repentance] those who have been once for all enlightened, who have consciously tasted the heavenly gift and have become sharers of the Holy Spirit,

⁵And have felt how good the Word of God is and the mighty powers of the age and world to come,

⁶If they then deviate from the faith and turn away from their allegiance—[it is impossible] to bring them back to repentance, for (because, while, as long as) they nail upon the cross the Son of God afresh [as far as they are concerned] and are holding [Him] up to contempt and shame and public disgrace.

—Hebrews 6:4–6 (AMP)

²⁵Now every athlete who goes into training conducts himself temperately and restricts himself in all things. They do it to win a wreath that will soon wither, but we [do it to receive a crown of eternal blessedness] that cannot wither.

²⁶Therefore I do not run uncertainly (without definite aim). I do not box like one beating the air and striking without an adversary.

²⁷But [like a boxer] I buffet my body [handle it roughly, discipline it by hardships] and subdue it, for fear that after proclaiming to others the Gospel and things pertaining to it, I myself should become unfit [not stand the test, be unapproved and rejected as a counterfeit].

—1 Corinthians 9:25–27 (AMP)

SUGGESTED READING

1. *The Real Faith,* by Charles S. Price, or (updated version) *The Real Faith for Healing,* by Charles S. Price
2. *Abandonment to Divine Providence,* by Jean-Pierre de Caussade

INDEX OF SCRIPTURE

INDEX OF SCRIPTURE

INDEX OF SCRIPTURE

To order additional copies of this book,
please visit www.redemption-press.com
Also available on Amazon.com and BarnesandNoble.com
Or by calling toll free 1+ (844) 273-3336

REDEMPTION❦PRESS

CPSIA information can be obtained at www.ICGtesting.com
Printed in the USA
LVOW05s0312230714

395515LV00002B/2/P